SUSTAINABILITY
AND THE
ABOLITION OF TAXATION

PHILIP RODGERS

MURTESS PUBLISHING

Published in Great Britain by Murtess Publishing

ISBN 978-0-9565704-0-6

First Edition

Printed in Great Britain by Dolman Scott Limited,
 www.dolmanscott.com.

FOREWORD

This book offers a radical approach to promoting sustainable use of the environment and of financing government by suggesting a means to achieve the complete abolition of taxation. In doing so, it also throws light on the ownership and husbandry of the resources of the Earth. The basic idea for raising government income will serve to ensure the conservation of natural and common-pool resources owned by everyone. It provides a method of reducing the level of poverty caused by market failure, and of freeing citizens from the continuing sequestration of their income by the state. It offers more citizens a way of gaining independence from government by letting them retain sufficient income to provide for themselves where they are able and removes some of the risk of governments failing to meet their commitments to care for their citizens. Many of the ideas in this book have been suggested before; a few have even been tried. Its novel contribution is to fuse them together into a coordinated plan of action and to highlight them as a complete system of government finance of particular importance to the age-old problem of eradicating poverty and the modern desire to conserve natural resources and protect the environment.

Philip Rodgers
May 2011

CONTENTS

SUSTAINABILITY

AN INTRODUCTION TO THE PROBLEM

Since the beginning of time people have been forced by the local warlord to pay for his keep. In spite of the tyranny that this has imposed there has been a benefit of sorts. Because the warlord has had a stake in the survival of his subjects, it has been necessary for him to offer them some degree of protection from others. As a result, tribes of whatever form have developed a communal defence structure against external forces. Further, to be able to pay their tribute, people have had to be prevented from fighting amongst themselves. Thus, a degree of law and order has had to be imposed. Of course, the subjects have had to pay for that too.

In some but by no means all parts of the world, through various attempts at civilisation, mankind has paired back the absolute power of life and death wielded, usually with great ferocity, by warlords, to impose a kinder form of government.

Yet, in spite of this growing civilisation, the use of coercive power to take money to pay for government remains softened only in that the retribution the authorities take for failure to comply has been reduced from death to mere imprisonment. It is a telling indictment of the modern state that its system of funding is founded on the principles of a dark past.

This book explores the relationship between the individual and the state and questions the need for the state any longer to extract tribute from individuals.

An alternative way of funding the cooperative functions that the state performs as the servant of its people is suggested and the nature and extent that these should take is examined. Thus, this book questions whether governments need to tax their citizens in order to pay for services for them or whether a better system which serves voluntarily to legitimise government activity is available.

The solution offered may be seen as a new perspective on public finance. It recognises, nevertheless, that where there are market failures, the state has a duty to intervene so that the age-old problem of the divergence of need and ability to pay is overcome.

Yet it suggests that, in fact, a great deal of inability to pay is brought about by the state levying taxes on the one hand and, on the other, bolstering the aggregation of resources in the ownership of those who have no obvious right to them. Furthermore, extracting taxation depresses the economy which hits the poor harder than the comfortable or wealthy.

In some ways, this book could be treated as an exercise in thinking about the funding of government and public services, but it is more than that. To dilute the principles its offers will provide no help in ridding mankind of one of its least popular and unnecessary burdens, taxation.

The first notion put forward is that if the government wants to exist it should pay for itself just as the rest of us have to pay for ourselves, and should not continue the tired practice of warlords of forcing their fellows to pay for their lifestyle. Taxation is a lazy way of obtaining funding government.

In reality, we cannot do without some form of government and as things stand governments have every right to impose taxation because no alternative means of funding has been offered. We do not choose to be part of a nation and no government actually needs to impose taxes. It does not matter that the taxes are spent efficiently or inefficiently, virtuously, immorally or amorally, on elevating mankind or preserving an unjust status quo, or whatever.

Even if the money were spent perfectly, however that could be defined, the state should have no need to coerce people into paying taxes. Removal of property under duress invalidates any consent given. At the same time, it is too simplistic to argue that it is a form of state theft because we do not give consent. Given the freedom of choice we would probably pay many taxes willingly without being threatened with imprisonment. The problem is that the threat makes it impossible to give consent, not that the state is worried about that.

Supporters of the current tax and spend system of public finance might argue that nevertheless the state gives something in return for taxes but the value of what is taken cannot directly be given in return because the government has to pay (usually an awful lot) for its own keep, including the costs of taking the tax. Even if it were, restitution would not exactly reflect replacement of the money taken because civil servants spending the money have a different perception of the best way to spend it from that of those people from whom the money has been wrested. Hence the immediate utility taxpayers derive from public spending is inevitably lower than it would have been had they been able to spend the money themselves.

It is important to recognise, however, that taxation has offered funding for the protective umbrella in which people can run their lives, careers and businesses. Yet it is not a necessity if social, political and economic stability is to be maintained. This book offers an alternative that provides for government expenditure, but reverses the flow of funds from government to the people.

Dipping into the wealth and incomes of their people is too easy a resort for governments in societies as sophisticated as those we live in, in the developed world, at the beginning of the twenty-first century. There is no longer any excuse for it.

The second notion and fundamental to the

argument is that the resources of the universe belong to mankind (and any other inhabitants if they turn up) as a whole and that those who wish to use them, whether for profit or pleasure, should pay everyone else to do so. By this means, wealth is not removed from its initial owners, will be shared fairly and will provide enough for a basic income for every person, eradicating the most extreme economically induced poverty.

It would be unkind to hold out the hope of abolishing poverty entirely because that could only be achieved, as far as I can determine, by completely removing everyone's freedom of action.

Leaving aside the psychological impact that might have and the effects on liberty, it is unfortunately something that has not proved physically possible, even in the most extreme socialist states. It would also controvert the whole premise of this book which is to offer people the choice of what to do with their own money.

There will be those who say that the best pattern of expenditure for society may not be the sum of the spending chosen by individuals. It is their responsibility first to define what they regard as best for society and then persuade every single individual to agree to it. Otherwise, we have no way of knowing what is best for society. What amounts to the best can only be a matter of personal opinion.

Thus, this book argues for replacing the blanket levies we know as taxation, tariffs and duties by fees for the use of publicly-owned resources. This will exert the constraints of the market on government behaviour and size. The government could spend no more than it could earn (or temporarily borrow and pay back from its earnings).

The third notion concerns the destination of the profits from selling the use of commonly owned resources. The collection of fees from the use of resources will absorb some funds. The government must retain some for central services, such as defence and provision for those who cannot look after themselves, but the resources which mankind owns, and the government would manage on its behalf, are incredibly valuable. There should be a substantial amount left over from what a government needs for central services and administering the system, for distribution as a rental income to the population.

Hence, the remainder could be dispensed as a basic wage, a resource dividend, for everyone in equal shares to rich and poor alike, creating a means of paying for central services that is not economically and morally destructive, and which encourages careful use of the world's scarce resources. It will enable more people to provide for themselves, reducing the need for state intervention.

Comfort can be taken in that the basic ideas here are not new and have been set out and to some extent even put into practice before. They can be traced back at least to Thomas Paine[1]. However, this book offers a thoroughgoing system which has never previously been presented for both the

---

[1] Paine T. (1796) *Agrarian Justice*, available at http://www.thomaspaine.org/Archives/agjst.html

abolition of taxation and a means of finding the funds to allow government to continue without it.

There will be those who say that this system is based on juvenile economics; that it is too simplistic to use for such a complex matter as funding government. However, the human mind needs to consider things as generalities. That is to say, to reduce the complex to the simple so they can be understood effect by effect. Indeed, excessive detail is frequently used as a means of diverting attention during argument. Complexity is the friend of the fraudster.

A resource dividend system is not an impossible dream which offers to create a huge deficit in government finances but there will be those who will say it will. They will use simple multiplications of current prices by current amounts to try to prove there will be inadequate funds to finance government, let alone pay a dividend to the population.

However, abolishing taxation will free the economy in such a way that calculations based on the current position are fruitless. That is why I have not attempted any. The market will determine the limit that government can have to spend, and democracy must ensure that as much as possible is distributed as a resource dividend.

Opponents will deride the system by directing attention to the current needs of government and suggest that the notion that something will be left to distribute to the population is untenable. Part of the value of the system outlined in this book is that government will not need to be anything like as big as it is today, and will not be the deadweight that it is, taking taxes and decreasing the ability of the economy to earn enough to pay those taxes in the process.

The system may also be mistaken for an extreme version of 1960s supply-side economics which held that if tax rates were substantially reduced, the stimulus to the economy would be such that more tax revenue would be received. Supply-side economics is intended to increase tax revenue. The resource dividend system described here requires all tax rates to be set to zero and tax revenue to be reduced to nil. It is not about increasing tax revenue for government. The one item of common ground between supply-side economics and a resource dividend system is that both acknowledge that reducing tax rates stimulates an economy.

The system is based on returning to the people what was taken from them or their ancestors often centuries ago by force. It is not inherently anti-rich. On the contrary, I welcome people being rich. I do not enjoy people being poor and do not believe that taking from the rich will, in itself, solve the problem of poverty. That has been part of the problem. Taxation has been justified on the grounds that it redistributed income and wealth to the poorer groups in society. It is a highly contentious claim.

THE STATE AND THE INDIVIDUAL

The Social Contract

The question of taxation and of funding the modern warlord has its foundations in the ancient discussion of the relationship between the state and the individual.

Social and political theorists have suggested that a social contract has developed in which citizens are supposed willingly to give up the right to defend themselves in return for the protection and services of the state. It is as if this were some voluntary agreement entered into freely by both sides.

The problem with this argument is that the social contract is and always will be an unequal bargain and the citizen is given no choice as to whether or not to make the contract. The only escape is to flee to an area where another government of perhaps a different complexion holds sway. The history of the world is littered with such migrations, proof enough that large numbers of people have found the contract unsatisfactory in providing the protection it is claimed to offer.

The social contract is so unbalanced in the relative power of the parties to it, namely each individual versus the state, that governments are usually sufficiently strong to be able to ignore their side of the supposed bargain when it suits them.

Even in the most developed systems of government in North America, Western Europe, and Australasia there are ample cases to show of the authorities abandoning citizens, for example, by failing to provide adequate policing but of calling them to book when they have resorted to extracting their own violent retribution.

If the social contract had any meaning, the authorities would have to be able to show that they were providing adequate protection before they could prosecute individuals for taking independent action but no court, a part of government, in any country would countenance such an argument.

This approach has a more insidious side too. Governments see it as their second duty, after collecting taxes, to maintain order at whatever cost and, if necessary, regardless of justice. They view it as a necessary condition to being able to collect taxes. In the streets, this has some virtue but extended too greatly into markets it is likely to be oppressive and as prone to catastrophe as no regulation at all. Persistent intervention in foreign exchange markets, for example, has always ended in tears and economic suffering.

The self-justification for maintaining order whatever the cost to the individual has its roots in the belief of a need for a leviathan, a philosopher king. This may be interpreted in modern day parlance as educated civil servants who know better than the common man, and whose duty it is to protect people from themselves for the greater good of mankind even if it damages some of them or their interests.

The history of the development of civilisation is not of willingness on the part of governments to protect their people, but of a struggle to force them to do so. The extraordinary thing is that people have had sufficient power to force governments to concede liberties, and occasionally rights. This is in spite of the power of governments tactically to pick off opponents one-by-one and to impose the most severe coercive pressure on others.

In the United States, the symbolic beginning of the struggle was the Boston Tea Party and the fight continued onwards through the Civil War in the mid-19th century and the Civil Rights Campaign in the 1960s. In England, it began with Magna Carta in the 13th century and has likewise followed a political and legal process also via a Civil War in the 17th century.

From the time of the Norman Conquest until the introduction of European Law, a British Subject had no rights, only privileges. In other words, the

English were only free so long as the civil service acting as government through the monarchy chose to allow them the privilege of being free. It was not a right. The British subject was only free because the monarch chose to grant the privilege and could take that freedom away at will. Gradually, from the time of Magna Carta, the absolute power of the monarchy was eroded by the introduction of liberties, but the principle remained.

This is no mere debating point. The rights of the state to coerce and therefore to tax underlie the attitude of the state towards individual action and the reaction of the state to it.

Democracy is the foundation of liberty and yet at the beginning of the twenty-first century its development is by no means complete. Democracy has never truly been implemented. Nobody has yet devised a means by which the people can actually govern. All attempts require some means of delegating power. This is done by creating legislatures, governments and judiciaries. Yet, in delegating, responsibility and to a lesser extent power, are returned to the warlord.

However, the imperative of delegation has left government prey to falling into the hands of those with only their own interests to pursue. It has also allowed the continuation of a self-serving Establishment.

The development of democracy has taken many centuries. It is obviously far from being a completed task. Each move forward has been a child of its time.

When Magna Carta was signed, the democracy that was to develop in the modern world was merely an infant in the sense that power was only just beginning to shift away from an absolute monarchy. By the time of the Reform Act of 1832, wealth (and hence power) was more widespread and the development of the Westminster Model in the 1870s reflected great hope. However, as the Westminster Model declined so have democratic aspirations. The electorate has become cynical, sceptical, and unhappy that what it perceives as desirable has not been delivered.

The British Parliament runs on the principle of redress of grievances before granting supply and this is probably a fair description of the hopes of all democracies. Yet government in Britain has descended into a battle between the media and government. Unelected journalists, frequently from elite universities, spend their time trying to trap Government Ministers, and the government spends its time and valuable resources trying manipulate the media in order to pretend that it is perfect.

Yet despite the apparent disillusionment among the electorate with government and politics, taxes as a percentage of income have continued their upward trend. Elections have not stopped the relentless growth of taxation. Government is levying ever-greater amounts to increase its own size and activity. Perhaps the disillusionment is because of this and a belief that nothing can be done to stop it. The abolition of taxes is the next essential step to revitalise and reinvigorate democracy because it will help to peg back unacceptable use of authority and provide a substantial leap forward in wealth. It will force governments to manage common pool resources properly, because it will be from them that they obtain their revenue.

There is a further vital point. Nobody was given a choice as to whether they wanted to be born into this world. No-one is given a choice as to whether they wish to be part of a state or not. It is not possible to move anywhere in the world where there is no state, though there is a limited choice of to which state to subject oneself.

Around the world, many peoples have not willingly entered the modern state, preferring a nomadic life. The state does not know how to cope with their presence. It is sometimes unable to collect taxes, to provide education and some medical services, democratic representation and so on, simply because of the absence of a fixed address but local farmers are frequently only too pleased to use their labour when the economy demands it.

This uneasy and unhappy relationship lies at the heart of the problem that faces modern government. The time will come when the individual can no longer be coerced into joining a state that they have not chosen, forced to pay taxes whose disbursement pattern they do not accept.

Thus while the question with which this book deals begins with the problem of financing government, it reaches into how the treasure is spent, and the rights of a government and its subjects. To do this, it begins first with the question of what government ought to do and then covers how to pay for it while removing the coercive element. This requires an understanding of the means and methods of ownership and an acceptance that the most effective and socially efficient constraints on individual and government action are usually economic, rather than ethical.

The situation has been complicated by the language used to describe the relationship between one person and the rest. The collective noun has become one of tyranny's best refuges. It enables individuals to carry out activity and then shift the responsibility for that action to a different legal person, a committee, company, or government, among others. Of course, in reality that legal person is non-existent.

The principle of vicarious liability is one of the curses of the modern world. It enables individuals to pass blame from themselves onto something that does not exist. For example, where a company deliberately swindles people, the company gets the blame. Yet the individual who took the decision to defraud, the one who carried it out and those who knowingly benefited, can often escape entirely simply by saying "It was the company".

There is really no such entity as a state or government but rather a set of ambitious or fearful individuals with powers delegated to them by the ultimate authority which they use in their own style and which they enforce by recourse to the common need to maintain a dynamic status quo. The use of coercion is backed by arguments of equity in contributing to and receiving from society.

The effect, however, is that people are forced to contribute towards things that they may well find repugnant; pacifists for weapons and armies, humanitarians for abortions, for chemical weapons, even the salaries and expenses of second-rate politicians. There are many other examples. Hence, taxation can be seen for what it truly is, a fundamental breach of human rights.

The Role of Association

The discussion of the position of the individual in relation to the state creates an impression of one against all, a hideously imbalanced contest where the individual is prone to lose catastrophically. In the extreme, the truth of this is self-evident but it is also only a part of the story.

Mankind, through society, has often been more clever than to allow the imbalance to persist unnecessarily. Instead, a powerful way to redress the balance has been found and used to great effect. As with most things people have devised, it has been used for both good and bad.

Essentially, the individual has turned against the state the trick it itself uses. The state is merely a group of individuals acting in concert, whether by choice or coercion. This is true of any corporate body, be it company, corporation, army, college, association, club or whatever. Each of these operates within explicit and implicit rules, within the complex social and psychological systems of mankind.

The individual has found the route of free association as a means of combating the power of the state, playing it at its own game. However, this has gone far beyond the simple contest, and covers many relationships between different groups each representing some particular interest. This pluralism developed before the modern state, probably within the extended tribe. It was the original source of the warlord and therefore actually of the modern state itself.

Most modern states are run by pluralist political systems where the might of the powerful interest groups frustrates (or occasionally succumbs to) the weaker ones. In some cases, strength and weakness depend on the circumstances, and always depend on the contestants. How free free association is may be questionable. Individuals grow up in groups of differing complexions, families, tribes, schools, gangs and the like and each imposes a constraint on action while perhaps offering other choices. Thus association, like so many things in life, offers both opportunity and constraint. It is the source of the power of the state and a means of countering it.

The Rights of Man

Jean-Jacques Rousseau started his famous tract *Le Contrat Social* "L'homme est né libre et partout il est dans les fers"[2]. In discussing the social contract Rousseau felt that, as civilised society had developed, the responsibilities that had come with it had caused mankind to lose its freedom.

To twist his meaning a little, it is more true to say that man is born absolutely dependent; dependent on another human being for feeding, warmth and clothing in the first place and subsequently for education as to how to survive and progress.

There is much to suggest that this process is a struggle to throw off the chains of social conditioning, and psychological and economic pressure from others, in order to assert something of an individual place within society. Thus the struggle in a lifetime progresses from dependence to liberty.

In these conditions, whether man has rights or not is hardly relevant if the social, political and economic conditions in which individuals find themselves deny the presence of rights or prevent them being exercised.

If the social contract is to have a true meaning then individuals must first have the option of accepting it, and then and only then be required to

---

[2] "Man was born free, and everywhere he is in irons", Rousseau, Jean-Jacques (1762), *The Social Contract*, Penguin, London, 1974.

adhere to it, knowing that the government representing society will equally adhere to its side of the bargain. Neither of these conditions exists anywhere in the world, not so much because of government policy, but simply because of the social relationships and differences in power that exist between individuals and between individuals and the state.

The mere process of growing up, of moving from dependency to being able to take one's own decisions, does not occur sufficiently quickly for liberty to be reached before the constraints imposed by the power of others take over. Strangely, as people grow they appear to want to exercise their adult freedom as a means of forcing others, often their unfortunate children, to toe a line.

If the line were simply socially responsible behaviour limited to ensuring that the rights of others were no more disrupted than their own, there would be no difficulty. Yet people in positions of power, parents, teachers, bosses, seem incapable of understanding the difference between the level of control that gives freedom and a level which results in suppression and repression.

The cause of this is fear, fear that underlings will get out of hand if not dealt with firmly but of course, that is exactly what happens if a gentle hand, then regarded as soft, is used. The practical difficulty here is that there is no obvious age at which an individual could be expected formally to accept a social contract. A child grows into society, having been given a set of standards of behaviour by those who brought it up. They can vary considerably. The ability to replace such conditioning by free choice may take many years to emerge, perhaps not until the parents or guardians are dead, and even then perhaps never. It may be that it is less stressful for an individual simply to follow others and to bury the cognitive dissonance created than to have to determine their own philosophy and views on life. Going with the flock is safer.

The upshot is that nobody is ever given a formal opportunity of choosing to join society. It is simply expected of everyone. There are many individuals who, nevertheless, refuse to join, but they are then regarded as anti-social or oddities. Their desire not to participate is often not tolerated or respected by those in society. Of course, many are simply those who want to shirk responsibility and yet take their social rights and it is difficult to imagine someone who could easily live in the modern world in a state of nature.

Here is the heart of the problem of an individual's relationship with society. Society is part of the individual's environment, and just as people have to cope with earthquakes, floods and storms, they have to cope with society, other people, surrounding them.

The problem of this symbiotic relationship lies as much with society as with the individual. The limits of tolerance are not well defined. Society is apt to regard those who reject it as being more in a parasitic relationship - this can even apply to those outside the norms of society, though they do not want to be, by virtue of being unable to find servile work when an economy requires less labour for the production of goods and services than the population can provide.

Society is prone to impose patterns of behaviour that have nothing to do with whether society is threatened or not. It has a way of converting norms to morality and of seeing change as a threat. It expects the individual to join it - no choice is offered - and to join on the terms it lays down but society has no way of dealing with those who choose not to join. Yet, of course, Thatcher was right to believe that there is no such thing as society - it is a collective noun which suppresses the identity and individuality of those it includes. Society comprises a set of individuals all of whom conform to a greater or lesser degree but always incompletely to a set of patterns of behaviour.

In practice, society is a system of control which is flexible enough to absorb rebellious behaviour; adaptable enough to change its norms, but so watertight that it can crush action outside itself.

Hence, the justification for levying taxes on individuals has an unsound foundation. People can only pay a fair price for something if the price is determined by a market where freedom of choice governs the behaviour of the suppliers and purchasers. The simple absence of free choice in joining society eradicates the dubious right of the warlord to extract tribute. What is earned by individuals belongs to them and they can only be relieved of it justly by their own free acceptance.

The Function of Government

There is no doubt that government can contribute substantially to the comfort of mankind when properly carried out. The question is of determining what exactly that can mean. In the 1970s a notion emerged which included among its precepts that government (and hence taxation) should be as small as possible, and idea steeped in virtues and vices alike, but it boiled down to little more than a re-statement of nineteenth century laissez-faire capitalism. The underlying assumption of that philosophy - that anyone can find work if they lower their wage requirements sufficiently - was debunked by Keynes nearly a century ago.

There is much to commend the desire to cut down the size of government, taxation, and hand-outs, but the premise of leaving the inherent inequality created by under-controlled capitalism as a basis for achieving these is untenable in a modern society. Government has responsibilities, even it is does not wish to live up to them or find the money for them.

The strand of minimising taxation is one that hit a note with the public, although its intention was to free resources to increase profits for the owners of capital with the intention of making wealth creation more general.

Those who are not capitalists have watched this with mixed feelings. A belief in the provision of essential services, especially of medicine and education, by the state to those who cannot afford them has a widespread following. Indeed, even the most capitalist countries offer some provision of this sort. The degree offered varies with the philosophical complexion of changing governments but the principle, nevertheless, is universally accepted.

The reason the principle of provision of services by the state is accepted is not so much that it is a fundamental of civilisation, but rather that government has depended on it from the time of the warlord as a means of controlling and pacifying subjects. What is more, a sickly uneducated workforce is of little use to capital.

The provision of defence against others is the primary public good that can be provided by government – in other words, defence and police forces with the necessary mechanisms to support law enforcement.

Settlement of disputes between subjects follows soon after but generally, this has to be paid for by the parties involved. Thus, it is a matter of determining the degree to which government should provide public services rather than a question of whether.

The factors that should be allowed to determine the degree of state provision of services are at the heart of the division of political theories.

Extreme capitalism has it that the market will enable the provision of everything according to its availability, at a price. However, there are some services, notably health and education, that some cannot afford. The question of need as opposed to desire thus renders capitalism inadequate to meet the needs of all mankind.

Socialism's solution is that provision should be according to need. However, this removes the market from allocation of resources but has never offered a better means of allocation in its place. In practice, the committee has taken over, a cumbersome mechanism prone to human ignorance, incompetence and corruption. It has removed the incentive to provide for oneself and one's own where it is possible and indeed in the extreme, actively prevented it, removing many liberties in the process. In essence, neither system is acceptable without substantial compromise, simply on humanitarian grounds.

Clearly, however, there is a trade off between what can and ought to be provided as a public good and the cost in tribute for the subject. The level at which these can be balanced is highly subjective.

In the United Kingdom, under Thatcherism, the question was asked of how to pay and expression was given vent that some did not want to pay for services they thought others could or should work to afford. This wheedled its way into the thinking of the National Health Service, questioning whether the state could afford to pay for dental treatment, for care of the elderly, and also whether a reasonable level of state pension could be afforded.

The great difficulty is that the principle of making one's own provision for these was not applied from a starting point of equality. It never could be. The inequality meant that some did not have the basic surplus needed to be able to invest in the future and therefore it has exacerbated the inequality and injustice of the point from which they started.

Socialist systems have attempted to pay for these services by diverting crucial resources, rather than by creating them through economic activity.

This is a classic misallocation. They have tried to address inequality by creating a state warlord which seized almost anything it chose, flying in the face of the natural acquisitiveness of mankind. Yet even in the most extreme socialist countries, the principle of ownership of private wealth has been accepted – not least by political elites in their personal behaviour.

Yet there is one principle which unifies every government of whatever political complexion that has ever existed. It is a belief that the state has the right to sequester taxes from its subjects. As with all the worst principles, it is universally accepted, widely hated, and rationalised by cant.

One will not go far along the road of complaining about the injustice of taxation before some sanctimonious soul tells you that you should pay it as part of your public duty.

Unfortunately, this is true at present because no alternative has ever been made possible. Equally unfortunately, these tax volunteers enable government to waste natural resources and leave the environment unprotected.

This book argues that if a government wishes to exist it should have to earn its living the way the rest of us do, by producing something that people need or want and selling it so that the market determines the amount purchased and the price, and compels the efficient use of resources.

That may sound strange at first but a government is just as capable of setting itself up to provide services and charge for them as any one of the rest of us or the companies we establish to do just that. In fact, it is easier than that because government reluctance or ignorance already means that, where it could be earning an income simply by managing resources properly on behalf of its people, vast amounts of potential income are overlooked and left uncollected.

Of course, government should restrict itself to delivering only those services that cannot readily be provided by private companies and individuals. One of the most important of these is managing the natural resources with which we have been endowed – the land, the air and the seas. For the use of some of these, which belong to everyone, a charge known as a resource rental could be made which the state could collect on our behalf. That would provide for their efficient use, care and conservation.

Much of the central role of the state in an economy based on such a principle is a management task. Its function will be to collect from those who pay to use resources and to distribute equally to those who own them. The government would act as the commercial agent of its owners, the people.

Beyond this, the main social functions of the state then become to defend a country, to maintain law and order, and to provide for those who cannot provide for themselves. This is less of a task than would be the case under the warlords' welfare system because every individual, including those considered economically worthless or a cost to the state by government, would have an income – their rental income from the resources they own with everyone else.

We have to be careful to protect this income from any local or national government bodies which might try to take it for their own purposes. Those who cannot care for themselves are most vulnerable because they cannot stand up for their own money as we, acting as associates, could. The rest of us have a duty to protect the vulnerable from the greed of a government Treasury.

The state will try to take all the income of the vulnerable supposedly as a recompense for looking after them and will attempt to extend the principal to all who do not work. It will claim that they too are a burden because they do not add value by production and that they are not entitled to receive the benefits of their ownership of the Earth's resources because they do not contribute to developing them. The maxim is always: Remember to distrust the state.

It must be remembered too that there will be those who cannot provide for themselves who have no relatives or who need so much care that their relatives should not be expected to attempt to provide it. Ensuring that people do not suffer because of the disability of others is as much a duty of the state as providing for the needs of those who cannot look after themselves.

The responsibility of government in this area therefore is no more and no less than to provide what cannot be provided by individuals caring for themselves. This means central functions are the prerogative of government, such as collection of resource rentals, disbursement of the rental income in the form of a resource dividend, provision of defence forces and some of the agencies of law and order, care for those who cannot care for themselves, the old, infirm, and some children, means of ensuring that unrestrained capitalism does not crush freedom, means of overcoming market failures, and the like.

It does not follow that all these can best be provided by central government. Many, notably in the health-care and education functions and provision of law and order, are likely to be much better handled locally where macro-economic considerations are unlikely to stultify compassion and common sense.

In essence, a state should be allowed to provide as little as possible, because it cannot be trusted to honour even what it has agreed or promised. It is folly to expect anything from government and is cheating to pretend that there is some system that would encourage government to be fair. The solution is to make it as small a sector as possible and the dependency of the population on it minimal.

It is not a necessary condition for economic growth that there is a strong stable government in power. In the second half of the twentieth century, Italian governments lasted on average only eighteen months and were notoriously weak because of the fissile nature of the coalitions that formed them. Italy also had the second highest rate of economic growth in Europe.

However, there is a role for the state. It is in the provision of central services to ensure democracy, justice and order but again payment for these can rest with those who benefit or cause the cost. For example, there is no reason why the cost of an election should not be borne by those who vote paying a fee to do so. In contrast, the cost of the criminal justice system should be borne proportionately by those convicted of crime (with a caveat that sometimes criminals themselves are also the victims and such a rule must be operated with compassion).

The basic rule here is that first a criminal might compensate the victim and then could pay for the agencies necessary to catch, convict and punish.

However, the criminal justice systems of most countries are hideously incapable of dispensing justice. You only need to pay a visit to your local courts to see people completely incapable of controlling their actions through lack of mental capacity being punished, instead of treated with the kindness their condition deserves.

Though I acknowledge that this is in part due to the inadequacy of mankind's knowledge of psychiatry at this time in the early years of the twenty-first century, the attitude of judges, who guide proceedings, could be a lot more enlightened.

Government has an important role in ensuring that markets function properly. This includes preventing the development of monopolies and markets where there are a few excessively powerful buyers. There is a problem here in that government is one of the worst monopsonists, or monopoly buyers, that can be found. The sheer size of government means that it wields enormous, undue power as a purchaser, especially as an employer, a purchaser of labour.

This can be witnessed by the way governments have ground down the profitability of the various pseudo-private agencies that they have set up in the fashionable trend of recent years. Supposedly intended to create a quasi-market using internal efficiencies, in fact these bodies have been squeezed to a level where they can only extract wages from government. There is no profit, and no return for the risk of being an enterprise.

Clearly, there is a very important set of functions for government to perform in the realm of preserving peaceful conditions in which the population can go about its business and thrive.

Unfortunately, governments have resorted to taking on activities that are best left to individuals and business. Often they cannot be blamed for this as they have only been responding to the demands of electors. Yet excessive faith in the strength and ability of government has encouraged interference in areas where government action can only mean a reduction in the wealth and well-being of the population.

The Responsibilities of the Individual

The laissez-faire capitalism that re-emerged in the 1970s has since been put into practice to a limited extent. It would treat people as if they each were business enterprises. This means accepting that there will always be those at the margin of survival. It deems those who cannot work to provide themselves with a living as pretty well worthless in economic terms. Taking this line is a serious mistake because it concentrates only on people's contribution on the supply side of the economy. Though some people may be of marginal productive value, they remain nevertheless an important sector in demand, including among them not only the sick, crippled or inadequate, but also many pensioners.

However, many pensioners who have worked all their lives for enterprises and organisations that did not provide for their employees' pensions have found themselves with only a small income provided by the state, despite being assured by generations of government that the state would provide a proper and sufficient pension. They had taxes deducted from their incomes that were supposed to provide for just that.

The brilliant idea behind the Welfare State

was that current liabilities would be met from current taxes. Of course, the minute it is decided to abandon this policy a generation is created which has paid for their elders' old age but will not find their children providing for them. Therefore, they have to find the funds themselves if they are able and end up paying for two lots of old age, their parents and their own. It is tough if this happens at a stage in life when it is too late to lay down a decent fund for old age but that is what has happened in Britain and elsewhere in the early years of the twenty-first century.

This demonstrates the greatest of all lessons that the subject should learn about their warlord. What warlords say and what they do varies according to current expedient and fashionable philosophy. The one thing you cannot do is trust the state. Civil servants spend their whole lives trying to avoid spending because it means raising taxes which risks the government being overthrown at an election. Spending on those who no longer earn their incomes means imposing unpopular taxes on those who do. The priority of government will never be to meet its responsibilities to the weak.

The whole situation is carefully balanced around the impact on votes at elections. There is a trade-off between avoiding increasing taxation and spending as little as possible on the one hand while appearing to the electorate to be compassionate on the other.

The notion of a contractual or moral obligation to provide is non-existent to governments, except in appealing for election to office. It is a question of finding the balance between appearing to be kind-hearted and taking the minimum of taxes. In between, however, comes the matter of competence and efficiency in spending the taxes demanded.

It follows that individuals should always try to provide for themselves. This of course is easier said than done but the more individuals can do so the better, not out of any belief that this is most efficient, provides self-respect, is close to godliness or any other self-righteous and sanctimonious philosophy but simply because governments cannot be trusted to honour their obligations to their subjects. It is the individual who suffers under the burden if they are foolish enough to trust a government to honour a promise to provide.

The test question, however, is how much can individuals themselves provide? Here the problems start, because ability to do so depends on wealth, health and intelligence. If any one of those is lacking then the individual may need assistance.

The plain fact is that not everybody can provide adequately for themselves. First, old people who have never had the chance or income to accumulate pensions cannot start now. It takes forty years, a pensions sector that does not go bust, and a government that does not take a person's spare money, to provide a pension. The clock cannot be turned back.

There are those unfortunate enough that they would never be able to provide their own income even if they were able to want to. It is the duty of society to provide for them.

Therefore, the government has a role in ensuring that a decent and humane standard of living is provided for those who cannot provide for themselves. The provision must be based on ethical treatment of humans but ethics are rather subjective.

There is no agreed position on the ethics of inflicting harm for a greater benefit. Often, the argument of the end justifying the means is taken as virtuous, a step towards the greatest good of the greatest number.

This standard is a basic marker but highly unsatisfactory in its outcome, overlooking the position of the smaller number.

Often beneficiaries do not compensate losers in the quest for a greater benefit and the implication of the untrustworthiness of government is that individuals are best to provide as much as possible for themselves. To have to rely on the charity of a government is truly a definition of The Unfortunate.

However, while individuals ought to try to provide for themselves, this does not in any way remove the responsibility from government to keep its side of the social contract. It merely acknowledges that in a crisis (and it does not have to be much of a crisis) a government will not do so.

The Intransigence of Poverty

The remark in the Gospel of St Matthew that "the poor always ye have with you" is an indication that it has long been understood that ultimately poverty cannot be removed, because it has many causes.

The question of poverty at the margin is a difficult one. Mass starvation caused by the disruption of the market distribution system by war is easy to identify and its cure is to end the cause. Poverty caused by sickness can be alleviated by an efficient state benefits or charity.

Poverty at the margin will always exist in a market system. Worse, charity can cause poverty by undermining an economic system which produces wealth. Providing something free prevents businesses from developing to supply it. Depressing supply prevents the creation of demand for labour, wages and profits. Africa knows this well.

The perception of the intransigence of poverty reported by Saint Matthew reflects an insight that was not to be set out in theory until Keynes showed nearly 2000 years later that an economy can settle at a position where marginal employees are not needed for production. Marx noted that the pool of unemployed labour served to keep wages to a subsistence level, giving all the profit of labour to the owners of capital.

In this sense, a market is a compassionless being. The labour market accepts those who are needed and has no concern for the rest. The outcome, of course, is starvation of the unemployed and their dependents unless by some other means, such as charity or welfare provision, income and wealth are redistributed, and according to Keynes even if the unemployed offered to work for lower wages they would not be taken back into the workforce until an economy expanded to need them.

There is a range of goods and services that people must have in order to survive, including water, food, clothing and shelter and others which humanitarianism has decided that people should have regardless of wealth and income – education and medical treatment, for example.

However, education and medical treatment have some problematic characteristics. They fall victim to a market failure that means that need and ability to purchase are not matched. Education and medicine are unusual in that they are relatively expensive and require a substantial proportion of income compared to other needs. That means that both have to be given free to some extent. Generally, this has come to mean a provision at a basic level, but there is no accepted view across the world of what constitutes a basic provision and many countries do not have the wealth or political institutions necessary to be able to distribute it, even in a limited form.

Where sophisticated means of providing them have been devised, as in Britain for example, the demand has been extensive and in medicine apparently beyond the level of provision that the taxpayer through the political system has been willing to give. Whether this is really the case, whether the allocation of funding by politicians has been mismanaged, whether the funds provided have themselves been mismanaged through lack of competition, or whether there is a philosophical reluctance to provide for the poor is unclear. As likely as not, all have played some part.

However, economics explains that if the price of a good or service is set to zero there could be almost limitless demand for it. Medical treatment certainly tends to show this, but there is only so much education a child can receive and as the number of children requiring education is fairly inflexible, limitless demand is not really a problem. Nevertheless, both these services would benefit from a market being able to operate where people could purchase them if they chose, instead of having to ask a state official for permission.

One possible, if simplistic, solution to this potential excess demand would therefore appear to be to enable people to make their choices as they would for other goods and services and to do that they need the cash. Once again, the principle emerges that the individual should, and should be allowed to, make their own decisions about what goods and services to purchase, and in what quantity, without the interference of the state. The individual should not trust the state to provide because when a consideration more important to the state comes along the individual will take second place and suffer.

The Responsibilities of Corporations

Shifting responsibility from individuals to a collective is nowhere more apparent than in the behaviour of companies and the reaction of the law to them. The nonsense has come to be accepted that a company can be charged with a crime.

How can a company commit a crime? It has no mind of its own. A crime is the result of an action, and an action must be the result of a human decision, unless it is a reflex action. The only entity capable of taking a decision is a living being. A company is not a living being and yet in law the principle of vicarious liability - liability of a company for the actions of its members and employees without they themselves being liable, has come to be accepted.

In society, the power of companies has come to be disproportionate. This has largely been the result of the pool of unemployment that exists within economies. A company has the threat behind its demands of employees that an individual can always swap places with another currently in the pool. Seldom does an alternative position exist where an employee could say to a company "if you do not improve my working conditions I will leave and you will not be able to replace me; therefore your output will suffer".

In addition, people can be replaced by machines. If a company folds, its resources will be deployed elsewhere, and the market will still be satisfied. If an individual loses their job, the social and personal implications may be manifold.

Right-wing politicians are fond of using quotations from the Greek philosopher Aristotle. He provides many insights which sound appealing but there is something of a problem with this that many may be inclined to overlook. One of Aristotle's great works, *The Politics*, was an apologia for slavery – but he was peculiarly perceptive to suggest as he did that men will continue to be slaves until there are machines to replace them.

A moot point for students of philosophy is whether people can sell themselves into slavery. In practical terms, people do this in a limited way through employment, forfeiting their time and right to make their own decisions about their conduct in return for a wage.

The extent of this loss of freedom is extraordinary and widely under-estimated. People in fear of losing their income, are apt to behave in ways that they would never dream of in their private lives, often for little more than a subsistence wage.

Given the basic principle that the only person an individual can trust is themselves, the question then arises as to what a corporation can be expected to provide for society and for employees.

The expectations of what companies should provide are best reduced to the highest immediate wage with the right of the employee to decide what to do with it. Unfortunately, a molly-coddling corporate sector has been created where there is now an expectation that companies should provide at least a pension fund and possibly medical insurance, education for children, housing and more.

In general, this is highly undesirable. Far from being well looked after, employees are tied into a tyranny limiting their freedom to move. Worst of all is the provision of pensions by companies. The funds are not independent of the company and not guaranteed to materialise (in as far as anything can be). Pension funds remaining within a company's books are not protected from the bankruptcy of the company. They remain available for the company owners to use, however ill-advisedly, and lose.

Provision of pension funds is important. Individuals often do not comprehend just how much needs to be put aside to provide for retirement. People have little experience of working out how much they need because governments have promised to make provision, thereby removing the incentive to learn.

Life Assurance companies have used inflation to disguise poor returns with large numbers sheltering low value. In addition, the period spent retired has been lengthening as life expectancy increases, but do not expect the government to allow that to continue. State-sponsored retirement ages will be raised fast in order to protect governments from having to meet the pension promises of the last fifty years.

The Government does not seem to be able to comprehend that as the economy grows at an exponential rate and as Aristotle's prediction becomes closer to reality, it would be possible to pay decent pensions. All civil servants work on calculations using the present as their base, so they easily conclude that a population living ten years longer will create a need for a huge increase in tax rates that the electorate will not tolerate. In fact, people need to set aside something like a quarter of their wages and salaries throughout their working life to provide a decent pension. This is almost impossible for those earning below average wages when the state takes a third of their income in taxes on earnings and purchases.

The responsibility of corporations might extend therefore no further than providing acceptable working conditions and an agreed wage.

There remains, still, a problem with company (or employer) pensions. It is of knowing how much to set aside and of employees again losing their freedom to decide for themselves. The solution to this would come with the provision of a resource dividend from resource rentals and this is discussed later. It is the responsibility of individuals to provide for a pension at a level they decide, not at a level the company or any other person or institution decides.

One further problem remains with pension provision. It is typical of this world that, at the time when savings have the greatest effect for later life, people are likely to be earning the lowest wages of their lives and are least likely to be able to save. There are also many Foolish Maidens and others should not have to provide for them.

It is therefore important that at least some of the income of the young be set aside in a pension fund before they even join the workforce so that they need to set less aside for retirement while working, especially in the crucial years when as young adults they are trying to establish homes and families. It is equally important that as much as possible goes to individuals. So neither government nor employer should siphon money from wages into pension funds, least of all still controlled by the employers, on the grounds of pension provision.

It is the worst possible investment strategy for a person to put all their funds into a single place. No honest investment manager would ever recommend such a practice and yet this is done as a matter of routine today with people's pensions.

Conclusion

This section has set out the argument that individuals should receive directly the full fruits of their labour, rather than having some taken in pension provision or tax. The principle is that others cannot be trusted to do their best for the individual because they have their own interests. By receiving a full wage the individual then has the responsibility for providing for periods of incapacity and retirement. Perversely, the state has taxed this ability away from the poorest and encouraged a questionable investment strategy on the part of those able to earn a pensionable salary.

ALLOCATION OF GOODS AND SERVICES

The Development of Markets

Trade in goods and services started originally because someone had a surplus of one good to meet their needs and a deficit of another and this was mirrored by a corresponding deficit and surplus of another person. Possession, power over the location and use of goods, enabled these two to exchange their surpluses, creating an immediate benefit for both in that each obtained something needed for something which provided no benefit other than in exchange. Both are enriched by the process. This is the basis of a market, and is the normal way in which humans have come to swap goods and services.

Markets ration supply by allocating to those

able to give equal value in return but the value is itself determined internally within the market by the degrees of supply and demand. The development of money vastly improved the efficiency of markets by separating the acts of sale and purchase thereby removing the tedium of seeking to find a double coincidence of wants.

Occasionally goods and services are given with nothing asked in return, as presents or charity, though a strict line of argument would hold that the satisfaction received by the giver could be measured by the value in exchange foregone.

This raises the questions; what is good about the market system, why is the market so persistent a means of allocating goods, and, where does the market fail mankind?

The market should rate as one of mankind's greatest creations. As a means of allocating goods and services, it is unparalleled and, without it, we would not have the standard of living we now enjoy.

It is all the more significant because it sits squarely within the fundamentals of human nature and has been such a tough mechanism that it has never been suppressed, despite attempts in wartime and by communist and other totalitarian regimes. Yet like anything else in this world, it is prone to failure too.

The remarkable achievement of markets has been to ration goods and services to a level where mankind obtains the greatest benefit from the use of scarce resources, but the difficulty with this is that the ethical foundation is limited, not least simply by imperfect knowledge. Demand may be affected if consumers know that a producer employs unethical practices. Supply will be modified by the wish of producers to appear humane to purchasers or at least by the fear of adverse publicity. Therefore, where goods or services are needed but there is an inability to pay, a person has to go without. This presents no dilemma if the product is inessential – a luxury car, for example, but it creates tremendous difficulties if the product is something such as food. It is quite simple and efficient but there is not an ounce of compassion in it.

In large parts of the world, Marxist systems attempted to suppress the market system and to allocate goods and services by other means. They never completely succeeded in eradicating the market but the willingness of so many countries to experiment with non-market systems of allocation suggests that the serious imperfections within the market system have appeared insurmountable to many.

When markets fail, they may do so for one or more of a number of reasons. It is possible for monopolies to develop as has happened in branches of retailing and in computer software. These can destroy a market by removing the competition that protects the buyer, though there are benefits from monopoly too, standardisation being a good example. Alternatively, the nature of the market failure may be such that over-exploitation of limited resources occurs as has happened graphically with the

American bison and is happening currently in many fisheries and forests.

It may be that humanitarian need and ability to pay are not matched. This unforgiving aspect of markets is most clearly visible in the classic examples, education and medicine.

The Virtues of the Market System

The market for every product has two groups of people within it; those wanting to buy and those wanting to sell.

The demand for a good from those wanting to buy will normally be inversely related to the price. At a high price, few will be willing and able to buy whereas if the price is low many may be both willing and able. The precise configuration of demand is determined by the necessity of goods – for example, food compared to a picture for the wall – and by other factors such as fashion and tastes.

Supply of goods follows a different logic. The higher the price the more willing and able firms are to supply the market. At a high price, many firms can supply because the less efficient firms can join in. At a low price, only the most efficient firms are able to produce at a profit.

Similarly, the precise configuration of supply will be determined by the cost of the factors of production, such as labour, raw materials and capital goods.

The price in a market adjusts until it reaches the unique point where it equalises the quantity of goods demanded and the quantity of goods supplied and where both buyers and sellers are satisfied. At that point the market will clear. Those would-be buyers unwilling and unable to pay the going price leave the market as do the firms unable to make a profit from supplying at the going price. Excesses or shortages of supply or demand will be removed. This also means that there will be no pressure to change from the going price or the quantity demanded and supplied in each given period. Of course, tastes, costs and the like are continually changing, so the market never quite reaches such a settled state but will instead be constantly hunting for the equilibrium by making small shifts in price as the quantities demanded and supplied change.

Those who are willing and able to pay the going price or more are those who participate in purchasing the market equilibrium quantity. Those people who are unwilling or unable to pay the market price go without.

Firms trying to supply to the market a greater quantity would make a loss since the cost of supplying would be higher than the price obtainable. Hence, there is a powerful market signal normally given to producers to tell them that they have reached the level of supply that the market can absorb and that their additional resources would be better used producing something else. Similarly, a firm trying to supply to the market at above the going rate will find its products unsold.

The important point in the context of this book is that the market is a valuation and rationing system and, by and large, a successful one that should be used unless it fails.

It is remarkable that this system of allocation is so widely accepted without undue resentment or envy among those who go without, and for most goods and services no better way has been devised of deciding who shall and shall not have access to a good or service. However, if the good in question happens to be food then a market has no compassion about depriving people of food if they are not able to buy through lack of income.

Not surprisingly, a great deal of political effort has been put into devising and experimenting with ways of allocating goods and services on the basis of need not only in the Communist world but throughout the West too. Perhaps only in education has a system been developed which works reasonably well. Medical services have proved to have ever-increasing and insatiable demand as technology improves, but the amount of education a child needs to be literate is relatively limited and has proved manageable.

The problem with education being provided free by the state is that the parent is not treated as a customer. This means that their wishes are not considered important but the paymaster, the state, has no special interest in the progress of any particular child.

Through the market, the tax system has been used to try to correct some of the problems of poverty by redistributing income from higher earners to the poor. The purpose of this is to shift demand so that at any given price more of a commodity can be bought if purchasers are willing.

When this succeeds, the quantity going through the market is increased but at the cost of a higher market price in the face of increased demand. Fewer have to go without, but nonetheless, there still remain those who cannot afford to purchase the good.

Some care should be taken as this offers only a partial analysis. If demand for one product is raised then because budgets are limited, in the short-run at least, demand for another good must fall to compensate. However, this is not the whole truth. The poor have a greater propensity to consume. That is to say, they spend a higher proportion of their income than the rich, who have plenty for the immediate needs of life and are able to save.

When income is redistributed to the poor, Keynesian accelerator effects take over as a result of the increased expenditure and the whole economy expands. This is of course a single stimulus to the economy and its effects will gradually wither away but leaving the economy on a higher plane than it would have been without the redistribution. However, there is a counter to this. Increasing the tax rate reduces the Keynesian multiplier so there is an effect in the opposite direction negating the gain. The relative strength of each effect is uncertain.

Neo-classical economists would probably dispute this argument on the grounds that reducing the income of the rich would make investment funds more scarce and expensive, lowering the return on capital and reducing the incentive to invest, countering the positive impact of the accelerator. Which of the two effects is stronger in magnitude (which is the important point for the growth of the economy) is unknown.

However, since the return to labour from economic activity is usually higher than that to capital it is probable that the accelerator effects would outweigh the disincentives and a nett benefit would accrue. Further the labour income effect is likely to be the more immediate, with the investment effects taking longer to emerge.

Whatever the shortcomings of the market there is no doubt that it is highly efficient. It suits mankind's temperament and has served us well. It will take a fundamental change in society to remove it and viewed at the beginning of the twenty-first century, that seems inconceivable.

The best way for mankind to progress is to use the market, since it cannot be eradicated and indeed has so many virtues in the incredibly complex task of allocating scarce resources that there is every justification for keeping it.

What must be recognised though is that the market is not perfect and where it fails, efforts must be made to ensure that characteristics are imposed by some dint of human ingenuity which will make it work. Poverty is partly a result of the market doing its job, but it is also the result of unnecessary acquisitiveness and human frailty. Worse, it is sometimes a consequence of taxation. Taxation takes from those who can ill-afford to give and has for centuries depressed the growth of economies and the development of mankind.

The Impact of Taxation on a Market

Taxes come in many forms. Among the most lucrative for the Treasury are those imposed on earnings and profits, and those charged on purchases.

The effect of income taxes on a market is to reduce the ability of people to purchase so that at any given price fewer goods will be sold in each period. The consequent lack of demand depresses prices. Hence, both the level of output and market prices are lower. The output of good and services with income taxes is lower than it would be without them. The market price is also lower and the economy is smaller. There is less demand for labour and, hence, incomes are reduced.

Some will argue that this is only part of the story, which indeed it is, because the government will spend the taxes. This has the effect of raising demand, increasing prices and output. However, the government will not spend the money in the way the population would wish. If it did, there would be no need to tax people. Civil servants simply cannot spend the money as efficiently as people would themselves because they are not spending their own money and different pressures prevail in such circumstances. Therefore, consumers will not derive the same utility, or feeling of benefit, that would be achieved were they allowed to choose where the money goes. The increase in aggregate demand is not sufficient to offset the initial loss even with the help of the increased propensity to spend brought about by redistribution of income towards the poor.

Purchase taxes, excise duties and taxes on company profits work in a different way. They raise the price at which each quantity supplied would have to be sold for a company to break even, since they are an addition to the cost of a good. The market clearing equilibrium shifts to a point where, in contrast to income taxes, the price of goods is forced up but they have the same destructive effect on output and reduce company earnings.

Again, there will be those who argue that this partial result is neutralised when the effect of government spending is taken into account. The effect of government spending will again be to raise demand, returning output towards its original level but increasing prices further. Yet again, the quality of spending by civil servants cannot hope to approach that of individual households husbanding their own resources so the impact is not neutral even on the demand side alone. The reduction in output means that the economy is constricted and incomes are lower because the demand for labour is smaller. There is a double effect of raising prices. In other words, wherever taxes are levied, appropriation by the warlord makes everybody poorer. This soon includes the warlord himself because the rate of output is reduced, incomes are held down and economic growth slowed.

The Impact of Abolishing Taxation

The impact of a resource dividend system on the market for goods and services would be far-reaching. It will not be able to remove the problems of market allocation of goods and services but it could significantly reduce the problem of poverty.

Putting extra money into the pockets of the poor by abolishing taxation will increase demand substantially. Removing taxes on company profits would lower the cost of capital to companies. Competition would compel them, though not completely, to pass this on to the consumer by producing their output at lower cost. Hence, they would be able to increase supply. The increased profitability of companies would make investment more worthwhile creating a wider range of goods and services to the benefit of the consumer

Thus, on both the demand and supply sides of the market stimuli exist for a market enjoying the abolition of taxation to expand to provide goods and services to a greater number of customers. This would be complemented by the removal of spending distortions and wastage introduced by government intervention. Fewer people would need assistance to purchase education, medicine and the other needs of life. The numbers forced to live in inescapable poverty would decline. There would be less wastage of precious resources and capital. Supporters of taxation might point to the fact that, unlike people, governments never save. This has the virtue of increasing the amount of expenditure in an economy but of course reduces the amount available for investment, since savings provide the funds for investment. The nett effect of this is complex and contentious but not likely to remove the benefits of abolishing taxation.

Conclusion

Among the conclusions that can be drawn from this section is that the market system remains the best means of allocating goods and services yet devised and should continue to be used. There are areas where markets fail, however, and mankind's energies should be directed towards correcting them for they are an important source of poverty. It is also clear that taxes always have a destructive effect on output, despite the fact that governments spend the funds they take.

THE EARTH'S RESOURCES

The Problem of Common-Pool Resources

It is easy enough to understand that the Earth's resources have an economic value. Where ownership is clear, transfer of ownership of resources, such as land, water, and mineral rights, will generally be accompanied by an exchange of money in the opposite direction. Where ownership is unclear, it is possible to take or use a resource without a financial payment. Yet this does not reduce its economic value.

One of the big advantages of private ownership is that it provides an incentive to the owner to husband a resource properly in order to obtain an income from it and to preserve its value, though the incentive is not fool-proof.

Consider a patch of grazing land. If the land is owned by an individual, they will be able to charge to graze animals on the land. Access to the grazing has an economic value because the economic rent from the grass consumed can be shared between the landowner and the owner of the animals rather in the way that the earnings of a firm are shared between the owners and the work force. The economic value of the resource will be reflected in the price paid to the landowner to be able to harvest the grass.

If it is a common pool resource, the owner of the animals will be able to take the product of the land, the grazing, free. Yet there is no difference in the resource, other than its ownership. The financial value, or price, payable is nil but the economic value is still there. Thus, where a resource is commonly-owned and no steps are taken by government to recover the value of the resource, its economic value and its financial value become divorced.

A market failure is created where the economic value remains and is taken by the animal owner for nothing. However, the financial value is nil only because no body exists to collect a fee. Not surprisingly, to make matters worse, free common pool resources are prone to over-use. Over-use reduces their productive capacity and so fewer animals can be supported. Then all the owners whose animals graze the land find themselves able to graze fewer animals than if the land were properly managed. Thanks to the failure of government to manage properly access to common pool resources like roads and land, everybody is worse off. This needs further explanation because the implications are profound.

There are many forms of resources which are commonly-owned, not obviously owned by anyone, or where the ownership rights are not exercised. Among these are roads, parks, commons, fisheries, forests, the atmosphere and so on.

Roads and parks are obviously commonly-owned. The ownership of the atmosphere and fisheries is less obvious. Often where the ownership is clear, the rights are not exercised. Sometimes people have to pay a toll to travel along a road while elsewhere, they do so free. Usually there is no doubt, however, who owns a road, but no-one (government) has claimed ownership of the atmosphere.

The market failure takes hold where ownership rights are unclear, as with the atmosphere, or where the ownership rights are not exercised. In economic terms that right is to charge people for using a resource that has an economic value to the user. If use is allowed free then the financial return to the owner does not reflect the economic return the resource-user gets.

People use roads to convey themselves or freight to another place where they can sell their labour, consume (such as enjoying a spin or visiting relatives), or sell their goods. There is an economic value in this because if the road-owner charged a toll many users would be willing and able to pay it. In moving goods from one place to another, a transport firm has to pay for the capital cost of its vehicle, the cost of the driver, vehicle maintenance and fuel. The payments are proportionate to the unit cost and amounts used. It does not normally pay for the use of the road. This is anomalous.

The capital cost of the road is paid for by the company and all other taxpayers by amounts sequestered by the government which are completely unrelated to the use of the road. The same applies to all other resources to which there is open access (by which I mean where no charge is made proportionate to use).

Normally a market sends a signal to companies to stop using a resource when the cost of another unit of it begins to outweigh the return, in other words, when extra output makes the operation unprofitable. The problem is that the availability of all resources is limited and should therefore be rationed. Rationing is one function of a market and is achieved by adjusting the price to the level where the quantity used prevents losses.

We have already determined, however, that something may have an economic value to a user without there necessarily being a financial cost for the use. Hence, there is no market signal to tell users to limit their activities to a level where the resource will not be over-used.

Needless to say, if there is enough demand, a free resource will be over-used. No individual is to blame because nobody has the information a market would provide to correctly ration use.

We can explain why, without government action, the roads become congested, the rain forest destroyed, fisheries depleted, and grazing ruined. We can predict that the atmosphere will be polluted by carbon dioxide emissions.

The solution to the problem of sustainability of resources comes from understanding that the cause of over-use is a market failure. It is here that there is a huge, almost untapped, opportunity for governments to earn an income instead of needing to impose taxes.

In order to counter the over-use of resources governments, in their role as custodian of the resources of the world, must enforce the rights of their populations to the ownership of common-pool resources and extract a proper economic rent. In other words, they must charge for the use of resources according to the amount used in order to ration, counterbalancing the immediate costs to the populace with the removal of taxation. It is important that this charge is directly applied to the amount used.

A fashion has grown which suggests that a better way to ration the use of resources is to impose taxation on the purchase of inputs. For example, in order to reduce carbon emissions, green taxes have been imposed in Britain on vehicle fuel. These will have no impact on saving the atmosphere from carbon dioxide pollution whatsoever. Why? Because the charge has been imposed on an input – fuel – instead of on what the government wants to control - the output, carbon dioxide emissions.

When charges are imposed on inputs it makes substitutes (of which there is an infinite number making it impossible to prohibit or charge for the use of every one) more economically attractive and they will be used instead, frustrating the objective of the input charge. With fuel taxes the response will be to use more fuel-efficient engines. The motor manufacturers are already boasting that they are doing just that. Such engines will not be used unless they are cheaper than their fuel-expensive counterparts. Hence the cost of motoring will fall and therefore there will be more motoring, increasing the level of emissions.

Even if the tax were to succeed, ownership of the atmosphere is not settled. With any common-pool resource, unless a certain amount of use is clearly allocated to each user by right, then unless every user adheres to the ownership rights, foregoing use for philanthropic reasons merely leaves the resource to be used by another. They cannot be blamed for using the resource because there is no market signal to tell them to stop. That is the very essence of the market failure. The same applies to car-sharing and cycling to work.

Not even a desire to conserve the earth's resources justifies taxation. Because taxes on inputs are bound to fail, such taxes actually contribute to the failure of government to manage resources properly.

The Earth's resources belong to rich and poor alike in equal part, yet even now in the twenty first century governments allow those rich enough to afford the other factors of production needed to exploit common pool resources to have access to them free without collecting fees which belong in part to the poor. They allow assets belonging partly to the poor to be used free. The enormity of the scandal of failing to collect the rightful fees due to the poor can hardly be overstated.

Instead, the poor are sometimes given state

hand-outs as if they should be grateful and, moreover, apologetic for having to accept them. Governments have no idea of the value of resources that are offered free for disproportionate use by the well off. We have nothing to tell us how much of the assets of the poor are wasted by government inaction in this area, wasted by government failure to collect their income.

Only by governments making clear the ownership of common-pool resources and managing them for their populaces by charging for their use can sustainability be achieved. These are inescapable pre-conditions to sustainability.

The Right to Use Resources

Ownership is a legal description of possession with certain rights and sometimes duties supported by society through the law.

For most of the Earth's resources, ownership has been seized by individuals or granted to them by warlords. Occasionally, the injustice created by such action is recognised but more often than not excused by the passage of time. Whether the seizure happened a long time ago or recently is immaterial if it continues to deprive people of their rights now. This is especially if it reduces their income. Time should not be allowed to override the rights of other members of mankind. Failure to exercise the right is no pretext either, if people were prevented from doing so.

All the resources of the Earth existed initially as common pool resources. Whether they were jointly owned by everyone or owned by no-one is a moot point but is irrelevant here. It is clear that the right of all to use them existed *de facto*. It is equally clear that they could be used regardless of the impact on the rights of others. This is a potential source of conflict and would be something that the warlord would attempt to regulate once strife developed among his subjects and if it threatened to disturb his ability to extract tribute.

The pertinent point now is that when someone acquires a resource for their own use everyone else is deprived of the opportunity to do the same. Thus, a gain to one is balanced by a loss to all. In itself, there is nothing wrong with this so long as the losses are compensated. The way we deal with this in modern society is for the individual to compensate the losers by making a payment whose size is agreed between the demander and the suppliers.

Of the resources of the Earth that have fallen into private ownership, land is the most obvious example, though there are many places where land is also recognised as common property. There are others, air for example, which are freely available and have not acquired private owners but note that governments are starting to sell the right to use the Earth's atmosphere through carbon permits.

Ownership of resources has become more widespread as civilisation has developed. Primitive tribal societies appear to depend less on the idea. Before the arrival of the European, the Polynesians had little or no concept of private ownership. They were taught it by the missionaries as part of the Decalogue – Thou shalt not steal. Among them, the New Zealand Maori are an interesting example of a group which has retained the notion that resources belong to the community. Notably, this applies to land, game and fishing rights whose retention they negotiated with the British invaders under the Treaty of Waitangi in 1840.

Sitting alongside the question of ownership is the important question of the right to use a resource; this is a different matter from ownership of the resource, since an owner can let out rights to use without foregoing ownership. Private ownership normally conveys such a right but it is by no means the only way to possess the right of use.

It is clear that at one time the resources of the Earth, whether they belonged to no-one or everyone, were freely available in more than adequate quantities to be used by a small population which had no means of exhausting them.

The development of the warlord has been the means by which resources and assets have been garnered by coercive means into the hands of a few. There have been advantages in resource management arising from this process. That is not my concern here, though it should not be forgotten or dismissed as unimportant because of that. Those advantages have been substantial but so too have been the disadvantages. It does not follow that private ownership at the expense of others is the only way to obtain the advantages.

What was available for everyone to use has been restricted forcibly, and the restriction has given a windfall to those who originally took possession of the resource. This windfall has generally been passed down under the principle of heredity. As others have acquired wealth through the market, they have often converted their assets into resources. Land, of course, has been most common in this process.

The fact remains that in the Beginning these resources were never given to any individual and no individuals were given the right to take them for themselves. Current ownership cannot be justified on the basis of past acquisition or the benefits of present law and order (which is merely an indication of the population being conditioned or coerced to accept a wrong).

Nevertheless, the forests of the world are now mostly farmland and we must recognise that the descendants of those who acquired the land have put a lot into creating their current condition. They have often been responsible for good husbandry within a system that they did not create and could not with their own efforts alone overthrow.

An argument has developed that suggests that ownership should be gained by use. This would be different from where ownership was granted by a warlord or his descendants, as has happened in most cases with land. This view applies to common pool resources that have not been or cannot be divided, fisheries being a notable example. Because a person has not used a resource do they lose their right to use it if they ever wished or needed to?

There is a strong argument here in favour of this argument, particularly where there are those who have rested their livelihood on the resource and who would be particularly vulnerable if they were suddenly to find themselves competing with large numbers of newcomers. It would be especially the case where the users had husbanded and conserved the resource in such a way that it could be claimed that there would no longer be a resource but for their actions.

Unfortunately, there are few if any cases in wild sea fisheries, for example, where such a claim can be made. In the nature of fisheries, the fleets have taken what they can get, trapped by a prisoner's dilemma problem of conservation, and all round the world have resisted conservation measures through their political representative associations. Had they opposed the measures on the grounds that they were inept which they mostly have been, there might have been some justification for this, but the resistance has almost always been based on a misconception of self interest.

Analogously, the argument could be made that a shopkeeper depends on a local monopoly, yet we leave them vulnerable to whoever likes to set up in competition. It is the way of the economy. Only, therefore, where there has been effective conservation by the users could a case be made out for ownership of a resource by dint of historic use.

Where users have fought for open access in terms of freedom to invest in production, they cannot have it both ways.

To argue in favour of private rights to resources being acquired by historic exploitation requires substantial evidence of sustained and effective good practice in their husbandry. Even then, it is questionable whether the argument is sufficient to justify the privatisation of ownership of common pool public resources of the land and seas. It perpetuates a wrong, the absence of a financial return from the resource for the current generation.

The Conservation Advantages

The removal of tyranny and coercion, and an end to economic causes of poverty are exciting enough targets in themselves to justify introducing a system of resource rentals and resource dividends. Yet added to these is the importance of conserving the Earth and its resources, as far as this is possible, until they can be replenished from sources in Space or until mankind moves to other planets.

By charging for access to resources, their use will be rationed in exactly the same way that the use of everything else that is sold through a market is rationed. This will reduce harvesting to amounts that are sustainable in the case of self-renewing natural resources such as forests and fish stocks. Resources that are exhaustible, such as ore deposits, will be used at the rate that brings the greatest benefits to society. Those that exist as a common pool, such as roads, will see congestion reduced and alternatives encouraged.

There is no doubt that asking for charges to be made for things that are currently free, despite the complete abolition of taxation, will provoke savage resistance, especially because the losers in the re-allocation of income that results will be the already rich and powerful. There is a terrible danger that politicians will fall under their control, if they are not already. Some partial measures such as road charging or even rationing – eschewing the market system – might be the unwelcome result, as a means of placating those who recognise the injustice and inefficiency of sequestration of income and assets by the state.

This system cannot be introduced in part, however, alongside taxation and physical rationing. If any concession is given to the continuance of taxation, markets will not work to set the correct levels of price and resource use and governments will employ this as a continuing excuse both for arguing against the use of the system and of course for increasing tax rates. Resource rentals would risk being raised to punitive levels.

The only way to stop a tax rate being increased is to abolish the tax and it is imperative that this is done as quickly as possible. If the changeover takes longer than ten years the public will almost certainly be being duped. The decisive test is whether the total tax revenue being received by government declines to zero, with perhaps the exception of protective import duties where other countries do not follow suit.

Note, however, that charging for resources will not be seen by government to cause the abolition of taxation. On the contrary, they will see it as a complement. Rather, it is the other way round. The abolition of taxation will force government to seek an alternative source of funding. Sustainable management of common-pool resources offers that source. The extent to which governments continue to tax their people will come to be seen as a measure of their competence in managing common-pool resources, including the environment.

Environmentalism

A trend of thought has developed which seems to suggest that everything on the Earth should be in a primeval state of Nature, as if mankind has no place on the Earth unless it too follows the ways of raw nature. This is entirely to mistake the very character of the Earth itself.

5,000 years ago mankind throughout the world suffered disease and poverty to the extent that life expectancy was less than 40 years. In the underdeveloped parts of the world, this still remains the case, but where resources are heavily used, people have a life expectancy approaching double that.

Like it or not extinction of species is part of the Earth's development process. The number of species that became extinct before Man arrived on Earth is colossal. This was not part of an evil process, an early indication of the Earth having a tendency for self-destruction, but an essential movement to the development of higher forms of life and adaptation to changes in the environment the Earth provides.

The Earth is constantly changing. Even if Man, the animals and all the vegetation of the earth did not exist, the Earth would be changing. The physical processes related to the Earth's position as a planet of a star with finite energy means that the Earth cannot survive forever.

Closer to home, the geography of the Earth alters continually as the tectonic plates move. Earthquakes are proof of this, and because the Earth's climate is created and governed by the distribution of land and sea, the Earth's climate is constantly changing too.

There appears to be a view that if somehow the Earth's resources are conserved the Earth will have an infinite existence, that the climate will not change and that everything will be sustainable forever; the movement of the tectonic plates will merely create changes to which Man, the flora and fauna will be able to adapt and nothing will ever need to become extinct. Nothing could be further from the truth.

With man and animals on Earth, the Earth's resources are bound to become exhausted. Many of the Earth's resources are not renewable and will gradually disappear. Thus if mankind is to survive longer than its planet it must find either a way of living permanently in space or other planets which will accommodate it.

Yet if we are to do this, we must use the resources of the Earth because we do not have a state of economic development at the moment which will allow Man to be independent of the Earth.

The extreme environmentalists' state of nature would thus actually ensure the demise of mankind. The sooner it is able to live elsewhere the lower the likelihood of its being destroyed by an astronomical accident or the death throws of the Sun, but to do this Man must use the resources of the Earth. There is thus a paradox. Mankind's survival depends on using up the resources of the Earth but if they are depleted too quickly it will not survive anyway.

This creates a race. Man must learn to survive away from the Earth but may shorten his tenancy here to do so.

Teilhard's Great Challenge

The sections above rest on the principle that all the resources of the Earth, its oceans, air, fresh water, land, flora and fauna, belong in equal part to the inhabitants of Earth.

They have set out the case that the market

system is most closely related to human nature as a means of allocating the use of resources. However, while generally, markets function well, failures occur in some major areas of resource allocation.

In addition, even where markets work without failure their nature is to limit exploitation to a marginal case. This creates a problem in the labour market because it means that there will always be those unable to make more than a subsistence living. Indeed, mankind's proclivity for procreation suggests that the market alone will not limit the population even to that point and that therefore there will always be starvation under a market system, however well such a system provides for the rest of the population.

The great Jesuit philosopher Pierre Teilhard de Chardin identified the problem in *The Phenomenon of Man*. Man, he suggested, had reached a degree of perfection in his physical development but the challenge now was to invent a social system that eradicated injustice and poverty. In other words, the human body is in essence a good machine for carrying us through life but the society in which we live is not humane and just[3].

In economic terms, the market system in which we live is inhuman because it always has the marginal case and beyond in the labour market and the markets for food and other essentials. Yet the marginal case is crucial to the market system because it sends out the signals necessary for the

---

[3] Teilhard de Chardin, Pierre. (1948), *The Phenomenon of Man*, Penguin, New York.

process of allocation of goods and services to work efficiently. It determines the subsistence level of wages and the number of people needed by an economy, a society.

Inventing a market system compatible with human dignity which does not depend on starvation as a limiting constraint to the size of the labour market remains the greatest challenge for economists in the twenty first century. Such a system must recognise the virtues of the market and the natural inclination of humans to trade.

Conclusion

Governments hold huge quantities of assets on behalf of their people which they could market. The question is whether people would rather pay to walk in the park than have a third of their income taken in taxes. The difficulty in persuading the public that the former is the correct system to protect the environment is that people have become so conditioned to paying taxes that they just would not be able to conceive that they do not have to.

Yet by paying tax people are permitting governments to allow the environment to be eroded. The only way to conserve natural resources is to charge for using them, but governments do not have to if they can provide for their spending by taxation. Taxation lets governments shift their responsibilities for the environment on to others.

CHARGING FOR RESOURCE USE

The Philosophical Basis of Charges

The starting point for the abolition of taxation is a recognition that all natural resources belong to everyone. Thus, if someone wishes to use those resources, they must compensate everyone else by paying to do so. This is the basic principle of the prescription given here to enable the abolition of taxation.

A user gains by exploiting a resource, but everyone else has lost, perhaps only an infinitesimal amount each, but a significant amount when all uses of resources are counted, because less of each resource is available to everyone else. It is only fair that a user should buy access to the resource from all its other owners. The price agreed will be best determined by a market, our usual means of valuation and rationing.

Thus, instead of filling the public coffers by coercing individuals and corporations to hand over arbitrarily-determined amounts of money, the first major principle of a resource dividend system is that governments will completely replace taxation by acting as agents for their populations and selling the use of common pool resources to those who wish to use the resources for their own commercial gain or private benefit.

All income taxes and taxes on purchases must be abolished. So too should duties on international trade, though there is a case for duties to be applied to protect national industries based on resource use where foreign states effectively allow natural resources to be used at less than their economic value by continuing to operate a tax and spend system of public finance.

Unfortunately, any charges made by the state have come to be regarded as taxation of some form. Whenever the state levies a fee and offers no immediate goods and services in return in direct proportion to the cost paid, that may be regarded as taxation. It applies to purchase taxes, value-added tax, import duties and the like. As people go about their daily business, often simply of making a living to survive, they are coerced into paying these dues.

Yet there are cases where governments make charges which can be simply regarded as payment for receiving a service, or access to something communally owned.

Governments frequently charge a royalty for the exploitation of natural resources. For example, the United Kingdom and Alaskan governments, among many others, charge a royalty on oil extracted from within their territorial bounds.

Thus, there is nothing new in the idea of governments charging for a good or service provided by the public. When they do they are not taxing, although they may be prone to abusing a monopoly position by over-charging.

Moving Resources to Private Ownership

Whatever the rights and wrongs of the situation, we start from a position where ownership of some of the resources of the earth, notably land, fresh water, minerals and to a lesser extent fisheries and other wild self-renewing resources, have been transferred into private hands. This affects more than the right of all to use the resources. It substantially removes everybody's right to share in deciding the future management of the resources.

Private ownership has frequently been good for the husbandry of the resource and for the prudent owner but only spillover benefits could accrue to society as a whole. It is conceivable that these external benefits have provided a greater return to society than would have been the case had the resource remained public as the economy may well have been given greater stimulation than would have occurred otherwise.

Like anything else in this world, however, there have also been many cases where private ownership has not led to good husbandry, perhaps for the same reasons of human frailty that mean that poverty can never be completely eradicated, or perhaps deliberately.

A private owner only needs to encounter a cash flow problem to be forced to forsake future income for a windfall for the present.

It must equally be acknowledged that public ownership and management of resources has been almost universally bad. There has either been no recognition of a problem, paralysis in providing action to combat a recognised problem, incompetence, corruption or a complete failure to understand the economic problem inherent in common-pool resources which encourages their destruction. All too often, hideously mistaken management has failed to protect and often damaged a resource and those trying to make a living from it.

Nevertheless, there is no other way for the resources of the Earth to be managed effectively for the benefit of all mankind than by their being owned by public bodies. Though these too are vulnerable to cash flow problems, they are at least subject to public scrutiny.

Private Ownership of Resources

The question has arisen as to whether common pool resources could or should be given or sold to private individuals in perpetuity, a right for which they would pay a rental. There is little question that there are some potential advantages, the incentive for good husbandry being among the most powerful. Allowing people to own or lease property in perpetuity encourages them to maintain it, because it has a value to them in exchange if they decide to give it up.

In recent years governments have come to learn that the first danger in selling off valuable public assets is of doing so too cheaply. This is as great a danger in a resource rental system as it is under the present regime of coercive taxation. Public auctions offer the best means of reducing the risk but at present only within the context of a heavily tax-distorted economy. Sales of a right for less than the term to infinity face similar problems but the risk of error is less permanent.

There is no doubt that those who currently own the freehold to land and their descendants will feel an enormous sense of grievance if it is taken from them, only for them to have to bid against others for the continued use of land which is an essential component of their businesses and as such their living. This grievance will have to be addressed, given that they have brought the resource to its current state of productivity.

It should not be forgotten, however, that the opportunity was given to them in the first place at the expense of others, and that others deprived of their share have been reduced to employment in these enterprises rather than shared ownership.

The most significant aspect of the resource dividend system described in this book is that it is based on the sale of the use of the resources owned by each and every one of us, and in retirement and old age, or in periods of incapacity, there continues to be an income.

Income no longer remains something that for most people is exclusively earned by selling their labour. Hence, provision for retirement and the like, becomes less of a burden. Everyone is converted, or rather, restored to being an owner of capital.

The question of ownership of resources is one that cannot be shirked. The most valuable land is actually in the great cities and, to a lesser extent, towns where the value of output per acre is substantially higher than in the countryside. Offices, factories and shops, if they own the land on which they are located, pay nothing for the use of the land, though they may pay taxes for occupying it. Many large farms have single owners who run the business working their land themselves. The family may well have acquired the land centuries before. They hold the land free, not paying any rental for it. All of these forms of business employ staff.

We have argued that the land truly belongs to everyone. Is it right that this situation should persist? What are the benefits and the wrongs?

There can be little doubt that a right to ownership of land in perpetuity encourages, without actually guaranteeing, that the land will be well-husbanded, so that its potential as a factor of production is maintained. Often owners in perpetuity can claim to have considerably improved the productive capability of their land. Consider the condition of farmland in Britain when it was enclosed 300 years ago or in the United States with its settlement by Europeans 250 years ago or in southern Africa 150 years ago. The farmers holding the land nowadays at the start of the twenty-first century can justifiably claim to have enhanced immensely its productive capacity by discoveries and improvements in crop rotation, fertilisation and spraying to control pests, weeds and plant disease. Scientific advances have also significantly improved harvests.

The situation would be different were the farmer a tenant. The economic incentive would be to reduce the land to some poorer state by failing to maintain it in order to minimise the costs of holding the tenancy. The decline of the productive capacity would be timed to coincide with the end of the tenancy. The land need not necessarily be, and probably would not be reduced to worthless because the tenant farmer would need to balance the savings in current costs during their occupation against the loss of future productivity to be endured by whoever takes over. There would be a loss in running down the productive capacity of the land beyond the cost savings.

The lower productivity engendered by tenancy means that the owner of the land would receive a lower rent than the imputed rent received by the owner-farmer because the tenanted land is that bit less productive. Clearly, there is a benefit in the owner of the land being also the farmer.

The wrong, however, derives from the fact that the workers' ancestors shared the ownership of the land. Their right was taken from them centuries ago against their will leaving them now to be dependent for employment on the new owners. It must be remembered too that the labour market ensures that where there is unemployment of labour the marginal employee is paid only subsistence rates of income. Yet the ancestors of the unemployed were equal owners before being deprived of their possession by a warlord.

Economists including Marx and Keynes have shown the impact of the threat of unemployment on wages, how they are depressed so that the economic benefit of labour goes largely to the employer. Thus a two-fold effect has occurred. The descendents of the displaced owners find themselves deprived of the rental from the ownership of the land where they continue to work and of much of the benefit from the remaining resource they own, their labour, owing to conditions in the labour market. Therefore, we have a situation where the rightful owners of the land have been deprived of their chance to develop a business and share in its returns. A new owner who was not a party to the original sequestration has willingly inherited or purchased the benefits, but has also carefully developed the asset, maintaining and extending its productive capacity to the full.

Great care is needed here. The populace has no more right to take away a farm from its owner than a government has to remove arbitrarily a portion of a person's income by taxation. The reason, discussed later, is that land is only one of the factors of production used in business. Thus a farm is much more than just the land on which it stands.

Systems for Renting Resources

Exactly how the products of resources are sold for use will vary according to the resource in question. Systems available include public auction by either the English or the Dutch method, sealed tenders, open tenders, sale at a given price, and so forth.

However, the basic principle is that whatever is available should be sold for the price that maximises social benefit thereby setting a market-clearing price and extracting the greatest return for the owners of the resource, the people, and the user combined. The market determines the fair shares for each.

In the early days of the system, as much use as possible should be made of the open ascending auction method of sale because of its transparency and because it removes the risk of the government miscalculating the value of resources by over-pricing or under-pricing them.

Over-pricing is not too much of a problem because a seller can always come down. Under-pricing allows the buyer away with an undue consumer surplus, and will lead to over-exploitation and the loss of the correct level of resource rental to the owners.

It is a serious risk because those who might be asked to set the price will almost certainly be able to envisage the value of a resource only in its current use in our tax-distorted and depressed economy. Selling by open ascending auction will also reduce the possibility of buyers paying over the market price and risking bankruptcy for an investment for which they cannot generate a viable return.

Hence, once the system for selling has been decided the next question is to determine the amount of a resource that is to be made available. Then it must be sold to would-be users at such a price that demand just equals the amount supplied, a market-clearing price. This applies to land, water, plants, forests, fisheries, wild animals, minerals and the atmosphere.

Roads, for example, could be owned and run by the government. It might be more efficient if they were sold off to private companies which would make a charge for their use. The private companies would have to bid for the rental of the land on which roads run (as well as initially paying to purchase the asset) and would need to be required to maintain roads at a safe standard.

One suspects that doing this would quickly lead to the replacement of the current haphazard and dangerous transportation system based on personal conduction of motor vehicles by a safe computer-controlled network.

Some care is needed with the meanings here. Where, ultimately, experience enables prices to be set in advance by the state (subject of course to periodic adjustment), the level set must not be that of the monopolist trying to extract the maximum for itself but must be the level that ensures the resource is fully utilised.

Roads, for example, are a common pool resource which is subject to overuse and the dreadful congestion that ensues. The way to remove the congestion is to charge for use of the road. This will either force the potential user unable to pay onto another transport system or prevent them travelling at all. It will also pay for new and better roads so that demand and capacity come into line.

The economic consequences of this are more profound than can be imagined but, putting that aside, the state (or the operating company) has the choice of either setting the price at the level which will maximise the sales of road use which may mean that the roads are not fully used or at the level at which the roads are fully used. In some cases, these two points may be the same but it depends on the responsiveness of demand to the price change.

Because so many people in the developed world depend on road use for getting to work in the major industrial countries, demand is almost certainly fairly unresponsive to price changes. A large price increase is likely to bring about only a small drop in road use. In this circumstance, a monopolist has the chance to maximise its profits by setting road prices at a level far greater than that needed to allow full road use.

This is normally undesirable from the point of view of an economy and would probably remain so under a system of resource dividend. However, as the rental should be returned to the pockets of the whole population research will be needed to determine whether setting a profit maximising price for road use is actually undesirable.

Much might depend on who operates the road. If it is the government, then the public gets the benefit of exploitation of a monopoly. If the government leases the road to a private enterprise then the excess profit might be shared between the private concern and the public because a company would be willing and able to bid more for the lease.

This raises the question as to whether the right to use some resources could or should be sold in perpetuity. The business wishing to use land could buy the right for, say, a year, a few years, or forever. If it purchased the right for a year or a few years there would be an inadequate incentive to maintain the productive capacity of the land. If the right were granted in perpetuity then the business would have an incentive to retain the land in top condition because it would maximise its resale value. If the right were sold in perpetuity, society would receive an initial payment and then the annual resource rental.

If the business became unwilling or unable to pay the rental then the right would have to be sold on. In this situation, the rental would be set by the state, just as a shop-owner might demand a rent of a tenant. The level of the rental will be set by market forces. If the state charges too high a rental land will be left vacant and no rental earned.

There is thus an incentive to set the rental at a correct market level, though whether this means a level which will maximise resource rentals or ensure the full occupancy of land again remains to be seen. The state, acting on behalf of its people, would be a monopolist owner of its land.

The amount the business could pay for the land would depend on the profits that could be earned from using it.

Despite the nice theory, it would be very hard in the first instance for the state to set a correct level of rent for the land because the market-clearing price is determined by human perceptions of what might be. Normally in a market, these risks can be minimised, though not eradicated, by knowledge of the history of the market but at first there would be no history here and the risk is considerable.

It is critically important that the use of a specified quantity of a resource is sold and not a licence to unlimited access otherwise there will be a race to exploit the resource which will quickly see it exhausted. This applies to roads, fisheries and forests, among others.

Selling a licence in this way creates an

incentive to the user to obtain the greatest possible return from the payment made. This is achieved by taking as much of a resource as possible regardless of the impact on congestion and future availability, since the user may not have access to the resource in the future. It is thus highly undesirable.

A further problem exists. Just suppose a giant corporation bought up all the rights in the world to air. Air is so fundamental to humans that there could develop a conflict between the enterprise wanting to use the air for production and humans wishing to breathe.

The prospect would exist of humans suffocating if not enough air were set aside before the sale of the right to the corporation. Of course, if the company went too far and suffocated too many people the market for its products might shrink. If you think this is ridiculous, consider the behaviour of companies when property they have wanted has been inhabited by natives. More explicitly, think of the Brazilian Rain Forest.

I can imagine considerable objection to this system from many businesses, prominent among them farmers and landowners. The basis of their complaint would be that no-one would pay the sort of prices for their products that businesses would need to survive. This would ignore the fact that the population will be in general an awful lot richer for at least four reasons.

First, people would not be losing roughly 40% of their income in taxation, creating an immediate two-thirds increase in disposable income.

Secondly, people would not have to pay for several large, redundant, Departments of State, which could be done away with.

Thirdly, the removal of taxation would end appalling distortions in the economy so that it could function more efficiently, creating greater wealth for any given level of resources employed.

Fourthly, as regards farming, food is essential to survival. As such, people have to buy it. Demand is very inelastic. That puts a lot of power into the hands of food suppliers to charge an adequate price. How different this would be from the present, where farmers pay massive amounts of taxation and then often have to exist on state hand-outs.

All these mean that the way we see the food market at present will have to change completely, but it is a great example of what those distortions have done to our economy, an indication of the damage done by continuing into modern times a system of government funding reminiscent of tribute demanded by warlords.

The same principle applies to companies wishing to collect rainwater and sell it to us, to those which wish to drill for oil or dig for minerals or to broadcast across the airwaves. It would also apply to the unspoilt areas of the Earth where society through its governments might decide that no price could justify the use of a rare or precious area.

Examples Relating to Land

At the risk of being repetitious, it is fruitful to consider some examples of the way the system would work in the case of land. They show some of the difficulties and the relative bargaining power of the parties.

- ### *The Factory*

The factory is built on land which we have claimed for all. Thus it prevents all except the factory owners from using that land. For the exclusive use of the land the factory owners need to compensate everyone else for the fact that they are no longer able to use it. This is no different from the idea of a single owner of land allowing the factory owners to build on it and extracting a ground rent in return. The difference is simply that in this book it is contended that no-one has the right to exclusive ownership of land. This is not to be mistaken for the right to exclusive use of it, which can be purchased from the owners.

- ### *The Service Business*

The situation with regard to a service business is no different from that of the factory, except that offices tend to be located on the most valuable land in the very centre of cities and towns. An insurance company, for example, occupies land perhaps as part of an office block in exactly the same way as the factory. If it owned the office block it would pay the government for the right of exclusive use of the land. If it rented the block or part of it then the office block owner would pay the government and take account of the cost in the charges made for the offices.

• *The Farm*

The problem with suggesting a charge for exclusive use of land is that there is an inclination immediately to think of the occupiers of large amounts of land and that they would have to pay large amounts of money.

In fact, farmland is among the least productive forms and the revenue that a government might collect on behalf of its citizens would be quite limited. It takes a very large area of land to provide a living for a farmer and his staff. Compare this with the productivity of an office block in a capital city, say New York or London, occupying a tiny area but feeding many. The ground rent on land would reflect its earning capacity rather than its size.

There are other difficulties too. A farm is not just land. Farming is an economic activity which uses the standard factors of production defined by economics; land, labour and capital. Therefore, the farm should be viewed separately as a business standing on and using the land. The business, to be complete, also uses labour and physical capital in the form of buildings and machinery among other things.

This is perhaps easier to understand by imagining a mobile catering stall that attends events. The catering business occupies a piece of land, a pitch, but at the end of the day can be towed off elsewhere, leaving the land it occupied vacant. The farm is analogous to the stall, a business occupying a pitch, but separable from the pitch even though it uses it. The farm is not quite as portable as the catering stall, but is it possible to move the machinery, animals, labour, and business acumen of the owner, everything in fact except the land and permanent buildings, to another location and still be able to meet customer demand.

By looking at the problem this way it is easy to see that what was acquired centuries ago, when exclusive right to land was seized and perhaps distributed by a warlord, was really only the land, not the farm now built upon it. Later seizures and redistributions may, of course, have also included the businesses using the land, but it is important to distinguish conceptually the land and the other factors of production that constitute the whole farming business.

The restoration of the inheritance of which the displaced workers have been deprived is to be simply achieved by doing exactly as is done with the catering stall – charging for the pitch. Recognition of the rights of the displaced inhabitants, which is everyone, does not require the farmer to be evicted. The situation can simply be restored by making the farm business pay for the use of the land and distributing the rent to the owners, everyone. Charging for the land is not levying a tax on the farm, however dependent the farm is on the land.

It can sometimes be difficult to calculate what the rental should be where there is no mobility of an asset. Nonetheless, the solution to the problem presents no particular difficulties. The rental would be the amount that the farmer has to pay to prevent an under-bidder obtaining the right to use the land instead. In other words, the use of the land goes to the person or company willing to pay the most for it. If the farmer were unwilling to pay for the use of the land, the situation would be no different from that where he was unwilling to pay for labour to work the farm.

There should be no mystery about this. It is exactly the same process as someone renting a shop. At the end of the lease, the shopkeeper and the owner of the premises negotiate a new rental. There is an incentive for the owner not to overcharge.

If the shopkeeper is unwilling or unable to pay the rental demanded they leave the premises. The displaced shop-keeper may choose to re-locate the business or to sell the business on to a new tenant. Otherwise, the shop stands empty until a new tenant agrees terms, which are likely to become more encouraging the longer the premises remain vacant.

Assume that a farm business belongs to a sole farmer. The land on which the business is built belongs to us all. Assume also that the best use of the land is in farming. There may be some value also for walking, riding and the like but we will assume here that the land is for agricultural use only.

The community could sell the land to the farmer for his exclusive ownership and use in perpetuity, but that is undesirable as it discounts the value of future earnings and leaves the community no control over future activity. Hence, the solution is for the community to rent out the land to the farm business.

The government, acting as the agent of the community, would then rent the land, initially by auction or tender, giving occupancy for at least a decent period to the highest bidder. Note that the farmhouse and farm buildings would be kept separate from the land in this. If the highest bidder were the occupying farmer, he would add the rental of the land to his other business costs.

If the auction were won by another enterprise, the farmer would have the option of selling up, either to the new right-holder or to someone else, or of reaching agreement with the new right-holder on a sub-let. There is nothing strange about such a system. It happens all the time with the rental of retail premises. Without agreement, the land would not be providing an income to the populace or with which to pay for the usage right.

Farmers might object to paying for the use of land that they currently use free, believing that the charges would drive them out of business. However, they must remember that they would no longer be paying taxes of any sort, freeing their income to cover the rental and that the rental would reflect the relatively low productivity of farmland. In addition, the community would be richer and not paying taxes either, enabling them to pay higher prices for farm produce.

• *The House*

We may now examine the case of the householder. This could be seen as the farmhouse in the case above or any ordinary house in an ordinary town. The property is built on land which comprises access and perhaps a garden. The land belongs to the community, and, as in the case of the farm, assess to its use can be sold. The options for the householder are the same; buy the right of occupancy, and if not, either reach agreement with the new right-holder of the land or sell up. Again, the householder will be freed of the loss from their income of central government and local taxes giving increased ability to pay the rental.

The existing occupier has the choice of a full range of options and the decision will be governed by the economic constraints that apply to all purchases. The amount paid will be determined by the market, and the income to the government, to be passed on to its client, the community, will be the amount receivable from the right-holders.

- ## *Roads*

The notion of paying for road use is not new, but it has been atrociously explained and people are naturally quite hostile. When the matter has been raised they have frequently been left wondering where they are going to find extra money simply for getting to work, this on top of the massive burden of taxes they already shoulder.

Currently, people live further from their work than they should because use of the road to get there is free. It is not true that people pay for road use by taxes because the tax is unrelated to their willingness and ability to pay the tax, the amount of road use at any given rate of tax at which they would avail themselves, or the capacity of the particular roads on which they travel to work.

Worse, environmentalists have jumped on the bandwagon and sought to have additional taxes levied on fuel in the mistaken belief that that would reduce the quantity of carbon emissions into the atmosphere. The discussion around road charges is such a mess that I must set out the argument properly – and remember, under the resource dividend system proposed here all taxes on fuel must be removed.

The notion of paying a charge for the use of roads relates to one of the most intransigent problems governments and the population face in the modern world. Those resources of the world for which there is no obvious owner, or where a government as agent of an owning populace, fails to make a charge, are at serious risk of being over-used. Where the resource is natural and self-renewing the potential over-use may threaten its very existence.

Roads are a common pool resource treated as owned by the state and maintained from public funds, but they lack the emotive problems of natural resources. Yet like exploitation of natural resources, use of a road brings an economic benefit to the user. It may enable a company to transport its goods to its customers. It may permit a person to travel to work to sell their labour for a wage. It may simply provide enjoyment in the way that going to the theatre or a fun fair does. Hence road use has an economic value.

For all of these services there is a return, some of which could be acquired by the owner of the road in exactly the same way that the owner of a country park might charge people for walking across the land. Few people object to the notion of paying to use a country park, but there is substantial opposition to paying to use a road. Because the government operates the charging system, it is perceived as a tax. The opposition, however, exists simply because there is no perception in people's minds of the idea of paying to use a road. They have enjoyed an economic benefit without directly paying a price for their use of it. This is an example of a market failure. It is the more sensitive when dealing with fisheries and common-property forests because if over-exploited they decline and may eventually be destroyed.

Everybody, to a lesser or greater degree, uses roads, so what is the point of charging? Does it not just mean that a lot of administration costs are incurred which do not need to be?

Roads belong to everyone equally. You may prefer to argue that they belong to no-one in which case the distribution of ownership remains equal (at none per person). You may alternatively wish to argue that they belong to the government – but who is supposed to own the government? In many countries, it is the populace. In the United Kingdom, it is the Monarch. In some countries, the owner remains a dictator or warlord. In this last group, people may have other governmental problems with which to concern themselves than worrying about being taxed, but, in free countries, roads show perfectly why charges for the use of resources should be introduced.

Although they are owned by everyone in equal part, they are not used by everyone in equal part. Hence, it is absolutely right that those who take more than an equal share of the use of a road should compensate those who take less. There are substantial costs involved in building and maintaining roads.

It is not right that those who use the roads little should, by bearing an equal proportion of the cost, subsidise those who use them a lot. This is true even when allowance is made for the fact that they may enjoy a benefit from others using a road, such as the distribution of goods which they ultimately purchase. By buying goods a customer contributes to the costs and profits of the supplier. Hence, when a firm employs staff, the customer contributes towards their wages.

Because road use is largely free once the licence, the tax disc, has been obtained, congestion results. The British government has learned the lesson that it is impossible to eradicate congestion simply by building roads.

Demand for road use can be expected to follow the same pattern as for most other goods and services, with increasing demand the lower the price. Hence, to reduce congestion the answer is to raise the price of road use.

Road pricing is an example of a standard economists' response to dealing with the problem of over-use that occurs where there is open access to common pool resources. A similar solution has been offered to over-fishing and destruction of the rain forest. Excessive grazing of common land was largely dealt with long ago by the Enclosure Acts.

The problem of road use and congestion relates to the external effects, externalities, that users inflict on each other. When you set out on a journey by road you first have to stop at the edge of the road to allow other users past before you can join the traffic flow. At junctions the same thing happens. You may be held up by another vehicle travelling more slowly and so forth. You cannot just drive straight out of your property to the destination at your chosen speed without looking. Each time you are slowed you are experiencing the effect of an externality and your presence on the road affects other users too. They also have to slow to avoid colliding with you.

If you have ever seen the police escorting an ambulance through a town, or a VIP convoy you will have seen them reducing the impact of the externalities by clearing the route, even to the extent of escorting their charge across red traffic lights.

So if there were only a single vehicle and no people on or near a road, the user could travel to their destination in the minimum of time. As each extra user joins they force not only themselves but those already on the road to slow down.

There comes a point where the road becomes so busy that the number of vehicles travelling the road per time period actually starts to fall. Indeed, many readers will have experienced coming to a complete standstill simply through congestion alone. Thus the throughput of traffic rises at first as additional vehicles join but each extra one slows the traffic a fraction until a maximum throughput is reached. Then as further vehicles try to join the road the throughput starts to fall and may eventually reach zero on occasion.

If we think of another service, a café, this decline in output does not happen. The café will have a certain capacity and once that is reached new customers will be forced to go to the competitor next door. Their arrival does not compel everyone in the café to eat more slowly. The owners will realise that they are not maximising their profit if people are being turned away and will raise their prices until the number of people coming to the café matches its capacity.

Hence the price to be charged for travelling along a piece of road will depend, among other things, on its capacity and demand. If the government charges a fixed price per mile across the country (as it has tried to do in Britain by adding taxes to fuel in order to reduce the use of the environment) that will prove futile and wasteful because capacity and demand vary from place to place.

With a resource dividend system people would have the money from the taxation they no longer paid and would have some choice as to whether or not they availed themselves of the use of a particular road, moved closer to their work and so forth.

A charge for the benefit of the public purse could be raised from the provision of roads in two possible ways.

First, as at present, the government could build and maintain roads and charge for use of them. Alternatively, a private company could pay a rent for the land over which a road ran, and it could build and maintain the road, charging for its use.

It is virtually impossible to exist in the modern world by remaining within an area defined by walking distance. This places the individual in the sort of situation that governments love. Anything that the individual must do to survive is prone to be taxed because it cannot readily be evaded by substitution of an alternative.

In Britain, every vehicle using the roads must display a Road Fund Tax Disc on its front windscreen. The name is a classic example of government deceit. There is no Road Fund. All funds received by the Government go into a single account called the Consolidated Fund. In order to counter resistance to the introduction and steady increase in the charge, the lie was given out that the funds received would be used to maintain and improve the road system. Because of government banking procedures it could never happen that way. Hence, money spent on roads cannot be traced to Tax Disc payments and whether more or less is spent on roads is unrelated to the amount of cash received by the Government for Tax Discs. Nobody in the civil service is keeping account of the amount received and the amount spent in order to ensure that the proceeds of the Road Fund Tax are wholly spent on roads.

However, nor is the Road Fund Tax a tax. It is a charge made for a licence for a vehicle to use the road system. As such, it is no different from buying a season ticket to a football ground. The difference is only in the necessity to use a vehicle on the roads – near essential if there is inadequate local public transport – but a matter of choice if there is, whereas attending football matches is essential to earning a living only for a few.

We must be clear, however, that the purpose of road charging as discussed here is to make a proper economic charge on behalf of the owners of the road – the public – for its use. It is not to eradicate the most severe congestion, *per se,* though that would be an additional benefit, depending on the level of price needed to reduce congestion to a tolerable level. There are two principal points at which the charge might be set.

The first of these is the price consistent with allowing the greatest use of the road while eradicating congestion, and where economic activity based on the use of the road receives most encouragement.

In many instances, especially out of town, the road represents a monopoly. In this case, the owner can choose to set the price at the level which produces the highest profit. This may be less than the no-congestion level of traffic or may actually be at a level where some congestion occurs.

Road use shows well the problem of unequal use of a resource by those who own it equally. Hence, it is worth considering in more detail the impact it would have in the event of the abolition of taxation.

Since the government is presently the supplier, acting as agent for the people, it would only be able to spend what the market allowed it to earn. The opportunity to misuse a monopoly position to extract the profit for government coffers remains, but road prices can be set either at a social level for maximum use or at a monopolist's level for maximum profit.

Though the monopolist's level is undesirable

and results in a deadweight loss of output and benefit to the economy, it is nevertheless limited. If the government pushes the price higher even than the monopolist's profit maximising level, it begins to reduce its income, so there is a constraint on the amount that a government can exact from roads. The government has to make do with what it gets. It no more has the power to demand higher fees from road users than a company can demand people pay greater prices for its products.

A powerful economic limitation to the size of government, known as the substitution effect, emerges here. While in the short-run a monopolist can control a market, the opportunity exists for alternative products and services, in this case other means of transport, to become available and competitively priced.

There is therefore an incentive to the government not to exploit the monopoly position for short term gain, but to adopt a longer view to produce the greatest possible growth and social welfare.

There is a significant environmental lobby that believes that all that is needed to reduce road use is to tax fuel. The concept of substitution effects explains why that would not work.

If it is not blatantly obvious that here in the early years of the twenty first century we have the highest levels of fuel tax accompanied by the highest levels of road use, then what is already becoming a clear response of the motor industry to the taxes? Is it not more efficient engines, faster cars to make use of the clear sections of road, and safer cars to reduce the cost of accidents in material and human terms?

All these are excellent examples of substitution effects and they compound the evidence that taxes on inputs do not control the use of resources. Fuel taxes cannot stop road congestion or pollution of the environment.

Private means of transport have many advantages. Cars enjoy a pleasant ambience, are there immediately they are needed so there is no need to wait at bus stops or for trains or planes and are warm in a cold climate. Lorries deliver directly from door-to-door with no need for time-consuming transhipment.

Despite these advantages, if road prices became too great then substitute forms of transport would be developed and used. It should be noted that if the amount of traffic on un-priced roads continues to grow, journey times will increase accordingly, raising the cost of travel and encouraging the use of alternatives.

Nonetheless, in some rural areas, there are often no alternatives to private transport and there is unlikely to be sufficient demand for them. However, in these areas the charges for road use are likely to be minimal. Governments may choose for social reasons to support the cost of these roads.

There are other considerations, too. The first relates to the necessity to travel. Some travel is an economic imperative, the most obvious being to shop (or have goods and services delivered) and to go to work. Road charging will force a change in where people live. There will be pressure to live closer to the workplace in order to reduce the cost of travelling to work. This is likely to cause a significant switch in employment, and perhaps in the price of housing which will become more expensive in cities and less so out of town.

From all appearances, the charges for road use are going to have to be relatively high if they are to prevent congestion and encourage the use of other means of travel. The inconvenience and apparent waste of time associated with sitting in a traffic jam have not prevented congestion though it is hard to know how much they have encouraged switching to the use of public transport. It is worst in the larger cities where the best public transport exists. Clearly, the financial and social costs of some levels of congestion are tolerable.

Conclusion

It is to be expected that there will be significant changes in the relative price of goods according to the amount of transport needed to get them to market. Local products are likely to benefit from this, which should please those who believe global warming is a consequence of trade.

The disruption to people's lives will be indicative of the appalling distortion taxation has created in the world economy but will be worth the trouble as everyone will be better off.

Taxation reduces output, makes people poorer, stunts growth and introduces economic distortions, changing which activities are beneficial and which are not. Worst of all, it increases the unnecessary powers of government and creates an ever growing, ever more demanding monster.

Introducing road pricing shows one face of these distortions in the effect that unravelling them will have. It may be that some of these changes are reversed as the benefits of abolishing taxation emerge. Some of a richer population may prefer to move to the countryside. Travelling further may not be so bad if congestion is reduced or decent alternative forms of transport become available.

This also demonstrates how all-pervading the influence of taxation has been and how extensive will be the restructuring of an economy once it is done away with.

The farming world and those in businesses in a similar position will view this with horror and it should be remembered that the principle extends through all properties from office premises in city centres right down to homes on a plot or in a tower block.

The difficulty with acceptance of the principle is that it will be viewed as an additional cost. The idea that all taxes will be abolished counter-balancing this and the other charges for resource use but still leaving a gain will be treated as a false promise.

There is some considerable justification for such scepticism as there is no doubt that governments will attempt to make resource charges an additional source of income to taxes, perhaps allowing them to lower tax rates. If they did that, they would make everybody even poorer than they have already done.

However, resource charges will not be acceptable to many. It is impossible to calculate just how the new system of charges would affect incomes. Since the whole idea is to remove economically induced poverty and to create an income for all, it follows that the richest will probably find some of their wealth and income going to the starving. The rich are powerful and with access to the media, a sustained campaign of media-fomented denigration of the idea is inevitable.

Opposition will not be limited to the rich, however. Anything that disturbs the status quo is disturbing to the mind also. The basic scepticism that this is yet another form of taxation, and one to be added to all the others will be widespread. It is a legitimate fear and one that cannot be underestimated by anyone who wishes to promote a resource dividend system.

The likely response of government will be to go along with the idea to gain electoral support but then to use it as an additional means of raising revenue alongside taxes. In other words, accept the scheme in principle but water it down. A few of the less controversial parts of the scheme, charging for car parks and the like, might be used. The final element of this would be an apology for not distributing a rental income on the grounds that it had proved insufficient to leave a surplus after government expenditure had been met.

Resource rentals are not a tax because they are not a charge superimposed on the market cost of the goods or services, such as a value-added tax. They are not deducted compulsorily by the state. They are not a slice of your income or wealth taken under threat of punishment. You choose whether you want the service provided and pay the owners, one of whom is yourself.

Nevertheless, even if a resource rental were a tax, first, remember that to work without distortions every other tax must be abolished. This is not an option. It is a fundamental principle of the system.

Another principle at the heart of this system is that the size of government must be reduced to a bare minimum. Every penny spent on or by government will reduce the rental income payable to the populace. That should change the perspective of politicians at elections. There will be a distinct desire to keep the size of government down if they wish to stay in power, instead of saying that they will be forced to put up taxes for everybody's benefit.

This section is based on the principle that the resources of the Earth belong to each person in equal shares.

It follows from this that any people or organisations wishing to use those resources must pay for their use and the recipients of the payment will be the owners – all mankind. The justification for payment rests in the fact that shares of ownership and use are dissimilar. Hence, the heavier users compensate the lighter.

The agent in collecting the funds will be the government but it must be allowed to retain only absolutely necessary amounts and the remainder must be disbursed to the owners for them to decide freely how best to use the funds. There is no question that this is the Achilles heel of the system.

The resource dividend system limits the government to the amount of money it can obtain from the market sale of the use of resources. Governments will try to appropriate the funds from the owners but they could be brought into line by a democratic system.

Nevertheless, the importance must not be lost of recognising that governments will do everything in their power to try to retain money and not to minimise their costs. At least there will be a constraint on the amount of money available to government because it will be at the mercy of market demand for what it sells.

A further principle set out is that inheritance of the right to the Earth's resources by the descendants of thieves and warlords does not eradicate the right to ownership of stolen property of the descendants of those who were robbed. There are many in occupation of land who will find this extremely distressing.

Care must be taken to ensure that they understand that they have no right to more (or less, if they suffered misfortune) of the Earth's resources than anybody else.

Equally, others must understand that a business built on the free access to resources is not to be confused with the resource itself. A farming business is not simply the land used. The land is merely one of many factors of production that comprise a farm. There is no justification for taking a farm from a landowner and attempting to divide it up somehow. That would be disastrous.

Equally, there is no justification for the landowner holding the land for nothing. It is an input to his farming business and he should pay the true owners of the land for its use. No wonder large landowners are rich. They have one of the factors in their business's production process for nothing. Owners of steel factories would love to get the metal ores free but they do not. There is no reason why farmers and those who use the other resource of the earth including grazing, fisheries, forests and roads should not pay everyone else for their use. With the abolition of taxation they would have plenty of spare cash to do so.

THE ABOLITION OF TAXATION

Introducing the System

Switching from the present system of compulsion to a tax-free system will mean that the myriad of distortions introduced to the world economy will have to be unravelled. There would be little point in removing a long term tyranny only to replace it with another that causes a catastrophic short term economic loss. Economic loss means suffering.

The principle effect would be to free industrial production and household expenditure. However, there would not be an even effect across all sectors of the economy or across all economies.

People are bound ultimately to be better off because the choices as to how to spend money are determined by the consumer, given the true economic cost of resources used to produce goods and services and not by a self-righteous guiding hand taking the resources of households and misallocating them.

Of course, a gradual introduction opens up the danger of producing a godsend for those in government treasuries who will see the system not as a replacement for coercively appropriate money but as a supplement to it, although they will pretend that they are on the side of abolition.

Their moment will come when unravelling the distortions begins to cause difficulties in some sectors of the economy. Then, supported in particular by producers who see a rise in their costs without regarding the offsetting increased prices they can charge and the steady reduction in tax costs, they will suggest that abolition of taxation is a little too extreme and cannot be sustained without considerable disruption.

The basic idea of the system is a good one, they will say, but it should be allowed to run alongside conventional taxation to permit more-efficient use of primary resources and allow lower tax levels. They will hope and expect that once that dilution of the principle of total abolition of taxation is accepted they can then allow taxes to return to their steady creep upwards.

Remember, the Government created the distortions in the first place, and the extent of the disruption endured at any given moment will be a consequence of the violence and incompetence with which it removes them to introduce the new system. The more skilled are politicians in power and their civil servants, the less will be the disruption to the economy.

Remember too, that one of the greatest benefits of this system is that the people who operate markets, that is, everyone, determine a limit on the amount of money going into public coffers. No petty tyrant can demand more and the less efficient the managers are, the less the public coffers will receive. There will be an incentive to the government to employ effective civil servants.

Some heavy users of resources will complain bitterly that a charge for owning access to a resource or a resource rental for holding a resource is just another form of tax. Why is paying for resource use not just another form of taxation? When I hire a car at the airport is that taxation? The answer is no because I am free to choose whether I wish to hire the car or not. I could hire the car for a single total amount if the hiring company offered such a deal, or I could pay an initial fee and then an amount for as long as I keep the car. These additional amounts are agreed in advance. No-one has to own and use a resource. Hence, it is not taxation, but simple purchase as with any other good or service.

There is here an international aspect. Countries or states are artificial creations based on various criteria but they cannot isolate themselves from the rest of the world of which they are a part. A sensible approach would be for the system to be brought in gradually over a period of years. One country could not allow the failure of another to adopt the system to interfere with progress to tax-free liberty in its own domain. Either the system must be introduced in concert by all countries or trade barriers to ensure equality of treatment between domestic and foreign produce would be necessary.

A system of resource dividends cannot really work in a country unless it first defends itself against those parts of the world which do not operate the system and which may well in consequence be taking more than their fair share (as determined by a market) of resources.

A country attempting to try the system would face great problems because its own agriculture might find itself being smothered by cheaper imports from elsewhere in spite of the extra health generated otherwise in its own economy. Imposing this system in isolation could only be done if a country protected its people and businesses by the erection of substantial import barriers with tariffs set at a level designed to equate the cost of imports to those of home produced goods which have borne the cost directly or indirectly of resource rentals.

Thus import tariffs would need to be set at a level consistent with the cost of production under a resource dividend system. This is the only situation where the continued existence of taxation could be justified.

Great care will be needed to avoid distorting international trade and losing its benefits. To set protective tariffs to the correct level would be a difficult task, but a flexible and astute regime would quickly find the desirable levels.

It would be terribly damaging to domestic economies if tariffs were used to attempt to gain an undue competitive advantage over foreign businesses. The idea is not to make local goods cheaper than their foreign competitors. The intention is to make the price of foreign goods reflect the true economic cost of the resources used in their production.

Again of course, enemies of the system would try to claim that such protective tariffs would be illegal under international law because they would be in conflict with free trade treaties.

All these treaties, however, permit the use of tariffs to protect domestic industries from dumping arising from subsidies and failure to charge the true economic cost of products. Anyway, the number of cases where such measures would be needed would surely be small because there would be few competitive industries abroad benefiting from the absence of taxation.

A more likely problem would be that countries adhering to the old unjust system would start to erect trade barriers, whatever international law says, to protect their old inefficient tax and subsidies system of public funding.

Nevertheless, the system could be expected to cause some disruption to businesses. Ideally, it would be introduced slowly over a period of years with taxes being gradually reduced accordingly. The problem with this is that governments and civil services would simply see the system as a supplement to their coffers and the poor subjects would find themselves with an additional burden instead of the removal of the age-old tyranny.

Redistribution of Income and Wealth

Defenders of the tax system will claim that without it, the redistribution of income from rich to poor cannot take place and that therefore, its continuance is imperative. This completely overlooks the dissipation of the wealth that takes place through the mis-management of common pool resources in which the poor have their share too. Taxation has been an easy way, once for the thuggish warlord, now for governments, to acquire the funds they need for their expenditure without having to work for it, without having to husband the resources of their peoples to best effect.

The plain fact is that we do not know how much the development of the world's economy has been held back by taxation and how much richer the world would have been without it. We do not know whether the inequalities in the distribution of income and wealth would have been more or less marked. We do know that the poor are poorer because of taxation.

The main problem with the notion of the redistribution of wealth and income under a tax and subsidise system of public finance is that it boils down to giving with one hand and taking with the other. It is hard to imagine that this could be better than abolishing the taking and offering a steady, if small, income.

The real answer to the question of redistribution of income, however, is that the current tax and spend system based on the free use of land by businesses and farms has led to the biggest redistribution of wealth from the poor to the rich that anyone could have been devised. That was the warlords' intention and from their point of view it has been a massive success. The poor have been kept poor to work for them and the rich have become ever richer.

Provision of Public Goods and Services

There remains the question of how public goods and services could be provided under a system where the primary destination of government income is a resource dividend. Public goods and services considered here are those that are owned by the state or community and used without charge.

Which are these public goods? Today at the beginning of the 21st century they include armies, navies, police, fire services, highways, and in some countries ambulance, health and education services, among others.

They also include the three arms of government - legislatures, criminal judiciaries, and the executive at various national and more local levels.

The first factor of importance is that the distribution of income would be entirely different from that today. The principle is that government should be left no funds other than those necessary to provide public goods where there is a market failure that means that essentials would otherwise not be supplied.

The government can earn its own income as an agent for the population by taking a percentage of what it collects for the people. The precise figure for this cut could be arrived at by competitive tenders from political parties or from companies willing to offer executive services.

One can conceive that a potential government would have to offer a specific percentage figure to the electorate and be constitutionally bound to it if elected for a term of office.

The underlying idea is that the money obtained by selling the use of resources is disbursed to everyone in equal part so that everyone has a chance to pay for the essentials of life.

This may reduce or remove the market failures currently present in the provision of health and education services. Whether these costs could be met privately will depend on the reaction of revenue to increased demand arising from the abolition of taxation and the responsiveness of supply and demand for each product to this change within these two huge sectors of the economy.

A more difficult problem arises in trying to deal with who pays for the defence forces, the police, fire brigades, prisons and so forth. Defence forces are something of a problem. Their cost could be removed from the resource dividend received by the population.

There are two difficulties with this. First, it means that a government has an excuse for not handing over everything except its administration percentage to the population. This means a continuing undue power in its hands and inefficient spending. It also means that people could continue to be coerced into paying for something to which, on moral grounds, they object.

This leads into the discussion of free riders in society, and is not a problem to which I can offer a solution here. Each case will have to be discussed on its merits. For example, either pacifists are coerced into paying for the army or they are allowed to free ride. If allowed to free ride, the number of pacifists is likely to rise dramatically.

The fire brigade could be financed entirely through insurance policies, again with extra support from neighbouring brigades being purchased, all still within the current system of moving fire tenders up and down to provide complete cover. The problem comes with those who decline to take insurance cover, or where the insurance company refuses to pay or goes bust. It would probably transpire that fire brigades would be legally obliged to deal with a fire and then bill the beneficiary of their services so it would need to be a legal requirement to have fire insurance. More simply, the cost of the fire brigade could be deducted from the resource dividend.

With the police, the problem is different. Up to a point, people could choose to have the protection of the police or not as they wished. A quasi-capitalist notion of competing police forces offering their services within a single area is likely to lead to chaos and is not considered further. People could pay for their local force by choice. Where greater expertise or services were required, they could be bought in by the local force Likewise, central services, such as computer recording and monitoring dangerous people, could be bought in.

Suppose somebody is murdered. The relatives might decide not to pay for an investigation, in which case a murderer would be roaming free, an untenable notion. Alternatively, the dead person's insurance might pay but, if uninsured, the bill would be sent to their estate. Why should the estate pay when the police have failed to protect its owner? Clearly, there is an unshakeable case for provision of some central services by government.

Conclusion

These examples show the extent and nature of the changes in thinking that could occur. I am not advocating them. I am merely trying to show how the provision of services could be re-thought if people were given more choice of how to spend their money instead of it being taken from them under threat of punishment.

There are far too many possibilities to discuss in this or any other book and will have to be dealt with step-by-step on an individual basis. I have included them because I am keen to show that funding government is not easy but that the difficulties are not such as would prevent a determined government from making a system of resource dividends work. As likely as not the best way to provide public services will turn out to be very similar to the present system, from public coffers, except perhaps in education and health.

There are many decisions that have to be made about the services currently provided by the state which could be commissioned directly by individuals acting alone or in concert, no longer burdened by losing a substantial portion of their income to government.

The more services are removed from government, the smaller the government will become and the greater will be the amount available to be paid as a resource dividend.

However, things could continue largely as they are, except with taxation being replaced by charges for resource use, in which case the resource dividend will be smaller.

THE RESOURCE DIVIDEND

Allocation of the Resource Dividend

The idea of the state dispensing to the populace funds it receives from hiring out the use of resources will be regarded by many as nothing more than a pipe dream. Yet this is already done. Each year the Alaskan government gives a cheque to every citizen for interest on the Alaska Permanent Fund which comprises oil royalties collected and invested. In 2006 the Citizen Dividend was $3269 per person, or $13,076 a family of four.

There is a significant difference between what is suggested in this book and the Alaskan system. Alaska collects the royalties, gives them to managers and disburses the earnings from investing them. Here it is suggested that the funds should be paid directly to individuals who could invest them and manage them for themselves or spend them as they choose. Given that oil royalties have a limited lifetime, the Alaskan system is wise, if paternal. The royalties arise because the state constitution claims the rights for the people of the state as a whole to ownership of oil and other minerals. Extend the thinking from exhaustible resources like oil and minerals to inexhaustible ones like land and it quickly becomes clear that there would be no need for state intervention in the management of the funds.

There are two possible ways to allocate the funds from the sales of a right to use a publicly-owned resource. These funds would constitute a resource dividend payable to each and every inhabitant in return for the use of their property.

The first way is to accord an equal share of the resource dividend to each person existing. The second is to award rights equally to the current population, and to allow them to be heritable.

In the former, each child born would automatically receive a right to a resource dividend which would, in theory, fall or rise with each birth or death. In practice, this would be impossible to administer exactly and so it would be necessary for a government to estimate the position. While there would be some loss of equitability it would be trivial so long as the government made a genuine effort to match the resource dividend to its true level and did not attempt to store up dividend to meet future liabilities or waste the money on unnecessary activities. The loss of equitability would also be negligible compared to that of the present day system of tax and spend.

In the latter, the heritability would mean that children would only share what was given to their forebears at some arbitrary point in history. Fecund families would see the resource dividend spread thinly while people with few cousins would see their resource dividend increase.

There is no obvious justification for choosing any particular time for allocation of rights other than at the implementation of the system. Worse, the impact would be to promote growing inequality in the share of the resource dividend received, as the world's population changed – amounts determined not by the existence of the individual receiving it, but by the actions of others over whom they had no control and for which they bore no responsibility.

There is a greater danger in this method of allocation, than in that of equally sharing resource dividends, that a government might try to retain for its own use the dividends of those who die without heirs.

Disbursement of the Resource Dividend

Under a system of resource dividend, everyone would have a basic income before they got out of bed in the morning. The only funds withheld from the proceeds of the sale of the use of resources would be those needed to pay the collectors, and those needed to pay for public goods and services that cannot be purchased individually by consumers.

This should leave a substantial set of funds available to be passed on to the owners of the resources – the people.

Further, the existence of the system does not mean that the redistribution of income, possible under a tax system, becomes unattainable. On the contrary, the very basis of the system is to give people back their capital so that they can use the proceeds as they wish. Were a government to decide that distribution of the resource dividend should be skewed towards the poor that is entirely possible and without the problems of a poverty trap.

This is potentially one of the most important features of a resource dividend system. If an equal dividend were to prove to be inadequate to remove poverty caused by the economy, the income could be varied, but this goes against the initial egalitarian principle of ownership of the world's resource. What would be decent and basic if this were done are arguable and there are many practical problems that militate against this approach including that of determining how much somebody qualifying for support actually has in the way of wealth and income.

Some might fear that providing a basic income would lead to an increase in delinquency with increased numbers of people having the means to avoid work. This surely is their choice. The reader is warned, however, not to assume that the income from a resource dividend would be relatively large in comparison to the level needed to survive, let alone sufficient to avoid ever working or trading. The resource dividend would be drawn from the residual funds after the government has taken what it needs for itself. Employment or business would be the means of supplementing that basic income. Individuals could thus receive a return from both their capital and their labour.

However, markets have a way of setting the price of goods equal to what people have available to spend. This will force people to earn more if they wish to meet consumer desires, possibly even for the fundamentals of life. This is no different from the situation today, except that everybody has a headstart. In the first instance, raising the ability to buy would merely increase prices when there is no concomitant increase in supply, but the secondary effect is that more suppliers can make a profit at the new price level and economic accelerator effects take over to produce a much-enlarged economy. These impacts are additional to those resulting from allowing people and companies to keep the share of their income currently wrested from them as taxes.

With a resource dividend there comes a significant problem. It is no use to assume that everyone is capable of managing their own finances. There are a significant number of people who cannot. They include the seriously physically and mentally sick, the aged and infirm, and children.

However, the fundamental principle should be observed. It is that all people are equal shareholders in the resources of the universe and should receive equal income from those shares. The only justification for departing from that would be to skew the payments towards the poor to relieve poverty further. At present, these economic payments exist, even if they are unseen, but they go to the rich.

Children's Income

The question of how to treat children in this system is an important one. First, it has to be decided whether children should receive a resource dividend or not and if so at what age? Then comes the problem of whether the child should be expected to pay for its own basic needs in as far as the income allowed.

Practicality rules that in fact children cannot manage an income throughout the whole of their childhood. Though children learn by being encouraged to manage small amounts of money, they are not capable of handling their affairs until they are into their teens. Indeed the whole problem is about more than just receiving and spending or saving money. It concerns the point at which children can take responsibility for the budget for their own lives.

If a child has an income, it follows that it should be able to pay for some or all of its necessities from that income but of course, an infant is incapable of making such purchases. Thus, the management of the child's income must be left at least partly to its guardian.

One of the dangers of providing children with an income is that their guardians will take it for themselves. In one sense there is a great problem here of whether the nuclear family is to be regarded as the basic economic unit of society or whether this should be the individual.

Some difficulty is presented because we do not know, at this stage, how much the resource dividend received by each person might be. In the beginning, it can be expected to be at its smallest because the world's economy has many tax-induced distortions to shake out and at first it cannot be expected to grow quickly in response to an end to the debilitating impact of leakages of money to the state.

Whether the resource dividend would be sufficient to provide for a child remains to be seen. An important consideration is whether all or part of a child's income could be put into trust to provide their pension.

To this end, it would be sensible if a Fund were established for each child immediately they were born and at least a portion of their resource dividend placed in it as it is received and made inaccessible until the age of majority. Such action would maximise the funds available to keep the child when it reaches old age because the earlier investments are made the greater the growth that can be achieved.

Money saved between birth and the age of 16 will have far more effect in providing for a pension than any savings set aside in later life. A unit of currency invested at 3.5% per annum real interest at the age of 20 would be worth 4.05 units at the age of 60, whereas it would be worth 8.16 invested at birth.

The early years are the ideal time to save and under the current system of taxation are the time when people have the least spare money to save.

I suspect that many people on reaching the age of 16 and seeing how much has accumulated in their personal pension fund will decide to continue saving the same proportion because they have a tangible example of how worthwhile it can be. Others will choose to spend it. It is their money to do with as they please.

Provision for Infirmity

The question of how to provide for infirmity can conveniently be split into two. The first situation is of cases where the individual is able to provide for the occasion of infirmity and the second, of course, is where they are not.

In the former, the individual will be free to make adequate arrangements for periods of ill health and for old age. They should do this for themselves because governments simply cannot be trusted to observe a social contract when it becomes difficult, either by philosophical design or by accident.

The best way to guarantee that people are provided for is to ensure that they have the means and then to allow them to make their own plans for their needs. This is by no means perfect. People will mistake and underestimate their needs, in which case there will be a requirement for careful foresight, advice and education about making adequate provision. Some people will prefer to enjoy today rather than worry about tomorrow.

A generation like mine which has endlessly been promised jam tomorrow only for even basic health, dental, and geriatric care to be withdrawn after supposedly being taxed for it for half a century, is especially prone to putting tomorrow out of its mind. Some people will make the mistake of putting all their resources into one pension fund or one medical provider only for it to go bust. There are many pitfalls; in any form of investment, even providing for health care and pensions, risks must be spread.

In the second case, there is no possibility of taking personal decisions. Some provision can be made by management of the income from the resource dividend by relatives, friends or guardians. The infirm will still be entitled to their resource dividend and care must be taken to ensure that it is not siphoned off by those managing it.

Of course, the government too will try to retain the funds, claiming that it is making provision, but it is not difficult to guess what sort of provision – bigger, unnecessary, government departments with extra layers of managers, all of course to look after the infirm.

It is, however, an important principle that relatives and others should not be expected to contribute towards the cost of caring for the infirm. The cost over and above their resource dividend should be borne by all of us equally from government income withheld before calculation of the resource dividend.

Provision for Old Age

Directly linked to what happens to a child's resource dividend is the question of providing for old age – a period of life that is lengthening as a result of advances in medicine. It will continue to do so although governments can be guaranteed to try to force people to continue working later and later in life in order to reduce government costs.

Based on the principle that governments cannot be trusted to honour their word to provide for those who have previously provided for them, it is an imperative that funds should be established outside the control of government to provide for old age by each and every individual. It is of course equally imperative that such funds are outside the control of companies or anybody else who might try to garner them for their own purposes and then risk losing them.

It seems banal to have to warn of ever-present threats, yet in the world of pensions the proverb "Don't put all your eggs in one basket" appears to have been all but forgotten. It is essential that funds be invested through several sources in a proper spread of investments for all the stages of life.

It is critically important to minimise the risk of losses through poor investment decisions, and the normal accidents and incidents that the world throws up. The risk is all the higher because managers of funds are not placing their own money (though they will still claim their fees even if they lose everything for the fund owner) and this risk must be minimised.

On reflection, it is astounding how people in the developed countries have allowed the state to coerce them into paying tax on the promise that they would receive a pension and care in old age. Even worse is that most have actually believed the promise.

It is almost as astonishing that people have naively paid into employers' pension funds where there has been no protection against the employer going bankrupt. I suspect that most thought that the money was being placed in a Fund separate from the companies' fortunes. It is deplorable that successive governments have allowed such a weakness to continue and positively encouraged it with tax breaks.

By the time earners have contributed huge amounts of money to the state and company pension funds, there has been little or nothing in the way of spending money left for people to put into a savings fund for themselves. Yet the state has now turned on them and blamed them for failing to do exactly that. If the state had not taken so much in tax in the first place there might have been something left for investing for old age.

As it is, even in the richest countries in the world, people are now again completely exposed to the ravages of financial deprivation in old age.

The greatest risk of all is that greedy governments will see small private funds as easy prey. Children or the old are incapable of providing a defence for their funds and the managers will be looking to their own interests. Only guardians could stand against a government but could easily be deterred from doing so by the usual threats. To improve the balance of power it is important that government is reduced in size and kept to a bare minimum.

Conclusion

Perhaps it is only fair to the reader, especially to those in another age, to point out that this book has been written at a time when a number of governments in Western Europe have tried to and often succeeded in welching on promises given to their citizens to care for them in old age, to provide medical and dental treatment free, and to offer an old-age pension which alone would provide a respectable standard of living. They have done it in a manner that has left large groups stressed and impoverished.

In the provision of pensions, these states have decided that they will no longer keep their promise to give their citizens a pension on which they could live in old age. This has generally not been done explicitly but has been effected by raising the minimum age at which the pension becomes payable.

Although their citizens paid into state funds by means of taxation, they have now been told that they should have made private provision. The point that these governments taxed away the ability to make such provision from large portions of the lower (not just the lowest) paid in their populations is disregarded.

The second of these relates to provision for incapacity in old age, which was supposed to have been provided by the state health services. Unwilling, though able, to provide the necessary funds for this governments have simply stopped providing care by ending the service.

It has been done in a stealthy manner. No announcements to this effect were made. It simply has been that as people needed care their relatives were told it was not available. The relatives have been too kind to leave their elderly to suffer and, faced effectively with blackmail by the state and the officials who applied the policy, have paid considerable sums of their own money and money they might have expected to inherit in order to provide what the state had promised it would pay. The effect has been that few were at first affected and the viciousness of the policy only slowly emerged.

Now in England, the authorities expect old and incapable people to sell their homes to pay for private geriatric nursing. When the whole of the funds has been spent, the relatives are then expected to pay from their own pockets or to take the old person home and nurse them. This usually falls on a female relative who is expected to give up her job even if her household has no other source of income. Thus, government has become adept at breaking the social contract by attrition.

In Ireland, distraught relatives have threatened to take their old people and leave them at hospital emergency units. What else can the poor things do when they have been so let down by states that taxed away their income on a promise of provision of care?

In Britain, successive governments have allowed an incredible scandal in the private provision of endowment assurance policies whereby owners have been told that they are not to receive what they thought they had contracted to receive from private assurance companies despite making payments for many – usually twenty-five – years.

Here people did exactly what governments said they should have done – made private provision, and they were robbed by small print in contracts. It has been acknowledged by the payment of some compensation that the wording controverted what the victims were told verbally by salesmen about the endowment being guaranteed. Faced with a simple fall in the general value of equities (for which it was their job to be prepared) these companies have been unable to meet their commitments.

This has happened after a long period of hopeless management of a poor spread of investments and being fooled into believing that investments were providing a good return when most of the return amounted to nothing more than corrections for inflation.

Elsewhere governments have arbitrarily raised the retirement age, so that people having entered a social contract to cease working at a certain age have been told halfway or more through their lives that the rules have changed.

The Social Contract is a most one-sided contract. In fact, it is a major tenet underpinning this book that governments are no more than modern warlords, intent on funding their own excesses and offering the absolute minimum of care and protection to their subjects only when it suits them. There is really no such thing as a social contract to which government is a party.

PROBLEMS AND REJOINDERS

Readjustment of Economies

There is no doubt that introducing a system of resource dividend and disbursing the bulk of it in equal part to the population will induce considerable readjustment in economies.

The world's economic system has been based on the powerful gathering for themselves the imputed resource rentals through a dubious claim to ownership resulting from violent or coercive behaviour at some time in history. By necessity, the poor have a lower propensity to save than do the rich. A shift of income towards the poor will therefore stimulate the economy, producing a greater than proportionate demand for goods and services, making everybody including the rich that little bit richer.

In addition, the spending pattern of less well-off people is different with a bent towards consumer products of a shorter lifespan rather than investment goods. While this will be reduced, it will not change a great deal and will again act as a stimulant to the economy in the short run.

Both these are transitional effects, however. Although they will shift the economy onto a higher growth path, the shift will only occur once and will no longer be there to be taken when it has been used, though that is no reason for persisting with the status quo.

Despite being a once-and-for-all effect, it is nevertheless, still a long term, indeed a permanent one. It will lift the world's economy to a new level and the effect could only reversed by the return of taxation.

There are other major effects too. First, the system makes huge areas of government redundant. Government is reduced to the provision of goods and services for the common good, such as the forces of justice, law and order, which are provided for the community.

Why, you may wonder, cannot everybody contribute directly to the cost of their local police through insurance schemes? The answer is that they could if they all would but there will inevitably be those who will not join such schemes. They should have a right not to. There are many good reasons why someone may choose not to join privately instigated community schemes. There may be question marks over the competence, intentions or integrity of the organisers or schemes, which is justification enough, but unfortunately, that leaves an opening for those who want to free ride. In these areas, the government will still need a presence. A primary benefit of the old warlord will survive.

There may also continue to be a need for the provisions of other services where market failure occurs. It does not seem to be an essential feature of an economy based on resource dividends that the rental income would necessarily provide sufficient for everyone to pay privately for all the services of which they wish to avail themselves. There is of course a continuing danger that governments will pounce on this as a justification for retaining taxation, retaining their power to compel.

However, many of the jobs associated with the tasks of coercing and subjecting the population will disappear. Of course, the tax collectors will survive, given a new role collecting the resource rentals, but vast unnecessary tracts of government will become superfluous and the staff will have to find new posts. There will be a lot of suffering in the form of worry and stress which will actually be unnecessary.

No longer hamstrung by the burden of taxation, the world's economy will flourish as it has never done. Even the growth created by the electronic revolution will be surpassed, because the resource dividend system opens the whole world to a life with no economic poverty created by the state, nobody taking away your wealth or income. The distortions in spending money to avoid taxation will be completely removed so that investment can find the places with the best economic return, not the second best return after avoiding the ravages of the warlord. In addition, spending will also be freed of distortions brought about by the changes in competitiveness of pricing caused by taxation.

There is another major advantage to the abolition of taxation. Currently, sections of the community avoid paying their fair share towards the costs of government expenditure. They do it by using tax havens, and slick lawyers and accountants, or by unrecorded cash in hand payments. Others receive perks. Yet all still expect to drive along the roads free, leaving those unable to escape taxation to pay for their maintenance and upkeep.

A system of charging for resource use can only be evaded by outright stealing. Just as travelling on the tube without paying is theft. The system puts into people's minds the clear notion that resources have to be paid for and that not paying for their use is wrong. Of course, tax evasion will end with taxation itself, but so will the idea that taking something and not paying a fair share for it is somehow commendable.

It will take several years for this notion to become accepted but slowly people will begin to understand and change their behaviour. They will not want to return to tax and spend.

When taxes are applied to goods, there is normally a two-fold effect. The price of the good rises and the quantity purchased falls. However, it is usual for the good not to rise in price by the full amount of the tax because of consumer resistance to a price increase, so some of the burden of the tax falls on the supplier and the sales revenue received by the supplier falls.

With the removal of taxes, consumers will be able to exploit their surplus to the full. Producers will enjoy their surplus likewise. There will be significant downward pressure on prices and output will increase; all this because of the abolition of taxation.

A country deciding unilaterally to abolish taxation will face problems arising from imports where the full cost of producing some primary goods has not been paid. Yet, imagine the impact on direct foreign investment where firms can set up factories and workshops and not face corporate taxes. It is conceivable that the economy would receive such a stimulus that the abolition of taxation could result in far more going through government coffers than at present.

These effects though true in total will not apply in every case. Not only government will face disruption. Those industries that have enjoyed resources free will find themselves contracting until they reach a level which reflects the true economic cost of their activity instead of the inflated level brought about by free access to everybody else's resources but both these effects are highly desirable. They will protect the Earth's natural resources from over-exploitation and promote stable production. One of these, transport, reaches into vast areas of economic life. The adjustments will be numerous though not necessarily large.

There will be those who suggest that this book simply argues for the replacement of one set of taxes by another. I have already answered that point. A tax is something that you do not agree to pay. It is taken from you under threat of punishment. Nobody will be compelled to consume the services charged for under a resource dividend system. People will have only a responsibility to pay for what they use.

A more serious charge could be that the system of funding government suggested here, namely that the government should have to earn its own living, is regressive because the least well-off will contribute a greater proportion of their income to paying charges than the rich. This would be because the poor spend a greater proportion of their income.

In a sense, such an allegation is almost true. However, the system requires that everybody receive a dividend from the activities of government in the form of a rental income which overcomes this problem.

With the present tax and spend system of public finance, assistance to the least well-off is governed by the principle that the tax system should be progressive, effecting a redistribution of income towards the poor.

This resource dividend system allows the poor to earn their rightful income from the assets that have been seized from their ancestors or mismanaged and wasted by governments unaware of the economics of common property.

As such, the poor will need a lot less assistance because they will have a basic income. The smaller the income paid in resource dividend, the more likely the system is to be regressive. There is therefore a heavy responsibility placed on government to keep state expenditure as low as possible to make the system as progressive as possible.

The redistribution of income and wealth towards the poor has been a major tenet of government economic policy in all but extreme capitalist systems and there will undoubtedly be those who see the removal of taxation as an ending of this objective. They must look further.

The resource dividend system advocated here requires that government extracts for everybody, including the poorest, the true economic value of assets that it has been prepared in the past to mismanage, assets whose true income has been handed to those rich enough to use them.

Because the government will have to earn its own living, it will no longer be able to waste the assets of rich and poor alike. It will have to make sure it manages common pool assets profitably and sustainably if it is to enjoy an income. The poor will enjoy an immediate increment to their wealth in the form of earnings from assets now to be properly managed to derive from them too an income.

Inflation

Enemies of this system of resource dividend will suggest that increasing the income of the poor without an instantaneous increase in production also occurring will lead to rampant inflation. This is a danger, but the impact of the cuts in government expenditure that the system incurs through the redundancy of much of government itself will offset entirely the effect in financial terms.

The inflationary pressure that may occur will be through the increase in the total ability of the population to spend, but manufacturers and service providers will quickly adjust their output to this, thereby dissipating the impact.

It must be remembered, too, that the abolition of taxes on goods and companies will, all other things being unchanged, produce downward pressure on consumer prices exacting a discipline on the cost of the factors of production.

In practical terms, the government could remove the risk of inflation by cutting and abolishing corporate taxes a little ahead of the removal of income taxes to allow production to increase before the growth in demand appears.

There will be significant benefits to be gained from people being allowed to spend their money as they choose, rather than having it spent for them by civil servants.

Expenditure by a third person cannot properly match the needs and desires of an individual, and is therefore certain to be inefficient and wasteful. This loss of social welfare will be substantially reduced.

This is not to argue, however, that the sum of individual behaviour is always better. There are occasions when society can benefit from the guiding hand of the state but it is very difficult for this to occur as the cost of administration must be overcome before any benefits can be felt.

There will also certainly be changes in the relative prices of goods, services and assets resulting from introduction of the system. These will arise not only from the more efficient expenditure shifting demand for products and assets to match the needs and desires of the consumer but also as a result of the increased income of the poorer sections of the population.

Thus, there are two potential effects of a resource dividend system on prices. The abolition of taxes on goods, services, and companies will tend to push prices down since suppliers in competitive markets will now be able to offer for sale any given level of goods and services at a lower price and still make a profit.

To the extent that household income is retained, untaxed, before increases in output emerge there will be upward pressure on prices caused by under-production in the short-run.

The Constraint on Government Spending

An important underlying principle of a system of resource dividends is that governments can only spend what they earn. The responsiveness of revenue and profit to changes in the quantity of a resource put up for sale by a government will govern the amount of the resource sold, not a decision by a civil servant. In order to maximise their income governments will have to charge the price which the market determines. Persistent government borrowing, storing up trouble for the future, will be constrained by sales of resources, rather than freed by being able to tax.

It must be recognised, however, that this system does not remove warlords. It merely goes some way to civilising them by constraining their behaviour to within what they can earn from managing the resources of the Earth prudently. Indeed, they maximise what they have at their disposal by offering the benefits to all mankind rather than taking them away.

There is perhaps a further constraint on their actions. It does not follow that, just because a government, the warlord, should be allowed to collect the earnings from the sales of resources, it should be allowed to keep them. On the contrary, the best way to waste your money is to let someone else spend it.

Even a government with the best of intentions wishing to spend money for the benefit of its people must waste money because it does not know and can never know exactly the wishes of its people, a disparate and shifting variable.

If somebody other than the owner of money spends it on their behalf they cannot spend it as would the owner and this results in wastage since they cannot do better than the owner would but can only do worse. Therefore, in principle, all the earnings from the sale of resources should be handed in equal part to the resource owners, the people. They alone can best decide how money should be spent.

The only amount to which the government is entitled is a percentage to cover the costs of collection from resource users and disbursement to the people, once essential public goods are paid for.

In fact, there is no reason why a government should do the collection and disbursement. It could be done by private contractors on the instructions of the government though this pattern of business has had a troubled beginning in Britain in recent years.

In the past, state-owned industries and utilities have been notorious for losing money. Under a resource dividend system the risk still exists that state-run enterprises will think that the public purse is a source of easy funds to pay for their incompetence but there are reasons why this should not happen.

First, the new charges will be applied to resources in common use, not for the doubtful benefit of decaying staple industries where for reasons of regional and employment policy governments have been understandably slow to allow the market to perform its ruthless function of matching supply and demand for the benefit of all.

Secondly, managers who tell the public that they have not been able to make a profit (usually from a monopoly) causing the resource dividend to be reduced, should quickly find themselves replaced.

In the early days of the system I fear that this will not be as strong an incentive to profitability as it ought to be because people have been so bludgeoned into accepting that they have to pick up the tab for incompetence in state businesses that it will take a little while for them to realise their power, but it will come.

Thus the requirement to make a profit and the responsiveness of demand to increases in price will serve as market-based constraints on the size and power of government, very similar constraints to those that have enabled private enterprise to deliver the standard of living we enjoy today.

Conclusion

The benefits of a resource dividend system arise from ending the stultifying loss of income in the form of taxation, even though it may be partly for things that people acknowledge need to be provided centrally. The system described in this book could continue to provide essential central services, but would ensure that, as much as possible, the market served to ration the use of resources in a way compatible with human nature and which would serve to use them to the best advantage of mankind. In addition, there would be a constraint on the size of government and the government would have to earn its own living just as the rest of us do. All this would promote efficient spending.

There is no doubt that the greatest difficulties lie in the transition from the current system of state coercion to one of choice of use of resources. Perhaps the biggest obstacle to overcome will be a disbelief among the populace that it could ever happen, so conditioned are people to paying taxes.

The past behaviour of governments will serve to compound this scepticism because it is almost certain that they will see resource charges as a means of supplementing tax revenues. They will just not understand the damage that taxation does to the economy and earnings. They will not accept that they could earn their income without existing in fear of a tax backlash from the electorate. It will take great determination and a rare and clever statesman to put the system in place properly.

EPILOGUE

All this is uncosted. I toyed with providing some idea of what annual revenue might be raised by selling access to common pool resources but realised that the impact of completely freeing the economy from the burden of taxation would be so marked that it is impossible to know how rich the economy will become as a result. Such costings would be little better than fiction and provide no more than a set of figures based on assumptions that enemies of the system would use to divert attention from the basic principle. This book is concerned alone with the basic principle. The minutiae are so vast that they could never be written down, even in many volumes.

Others have made a stab, but the figures fail on several counts to reach what could be achieved with the thoroughgoing system described here. First, they usually leave out the potential revenue from the most valuable resources, land and thoroughfares. Secondly, they assume that revenue can be disbursed while retaining taxation. Thirdly, they miss the gains to be made from freeing the economy from the depressing effect of taxation. Fourthly, they omit the reaction of the economy to the comprehensive removal of tax-induced distortions. And so on. Yet the Alaskan Citizen Dividend has shown that it is possible to move in the right direction.

People have been brought up to accept the inevitability of their income or assets being taken by the state, under threat of punishment. It will take a few years for them to come to terms with a system of order that places the state in the position of servant. The populace will no longer be so readily bullied and coerced into handing over more than a third of its income to those who have little incentive to spend it wisely (a highly subjective concept) and who do not know how the owners of the money would have spent it.

People will have to get used to the idea that they should pay for the use of commonly-owned goods and services in accordance with the amount they use. Provision of goods and services free, invites their over-use and can only be justified where the administrative cost of collecting fees is greater than the fees generated but in those circumstances there is a question mark over whether the good or service should be provided at all. It depends on the particular good or service.

Remarkably, the resource dividend system offers a means of providing a small income for all and, at the same time, of meeting the brilliant concept of the welfare state set up in Britain with the support of all the political parties immediately after the Second World War of meeting current costs from current income.

By substantially dismantling the powers of government and by offering people the choice of how to spend their own money considerable liberalisation can take place without the violent impact on those who fall foul of the market.

A belief that the resources of the world belong to all mankind in equal share is not fundamental to the abolition of taxation. The same case, that governments are neglecting their duty to manage resources properly by allowing excessive and often free access to them can be made out whether the resources are commonly-owned, or owned by a monarch, the state or a private individual. It does provide a foundation for the payment of a resource dividend to all.

A resource dividend system does not protect individuals from financial shocks. Those must be covered as part of a prudent approach to spending and investment. The right to a continuing resource dividend must not be allowed to become heritable. The right must be born and die with a person otherwise the equality it recognises will be destroyed and in time an underclass re-created. It must not be acquired by their partners, children or other dependents, though of course any wealth accumulated from the resource dividend will be passed on by means of the normal rules of heredity.

Depending on society's choice made through the political system, the inability of the resource dividend to be inherited by a spouse could mean that half the basic household income is lost when someone is widowed, if no other provision has been made privately. However, it is better to know that the state will not cover such events than to have been told all one's life that the state will provide, only to find that the contract is to be broken when the promise is called in.

It will be argued that a rental income system is nothing more than the usual Treasury Minister's trick of giving with one hand and taking with the other. Nothing could be further from the truth. People will be able to keep the 30% to 40% of their income taken by the state but find themselves having to pay extra for food and travel, among other things. Yet to accept that as sufficient to reject the system belies the true impact. The eradication of distortions in spending means that every penny will be worth more and will encourage more-rapid growth in incomes. The income derived from the resource rentals will give many more the chance to live without handouts from the state and to decide on their own medical and educational provisions.

There will be a major redistribution of income. If some of the rich are worse off as a result, it will be because they can no longer go on receiving free the benefits of some of the world's resources at the expense of the poor, who also own a share in them. It is to be hoped that they will understand that the market says that their new level of income is what they are worth.

There is no socialist spite or envy involved; it is simply the removal of a distortion in the markets. There is a world of difference between saying "You have been enjoying the use of everybody's property free, but from now on you will pay properly for it" and saying "I don't want you to be rich". The latter is a reprehensible approach.

Yet the most serious danger is that governments will see this system as a way of raising additional money without opening the government to criticism for raising taxes. If that is done the impact will be to reduce the capacity of the economy to grow and therefore to make the whole population poorer. For the system to work, people must have the means to pay for the use of common pool resources created by allowing them to keep their own money. It is equally important that government be cut down to meet its new limited role. Failure to maximise the ratio of the amount of the resource dividend distributed to that retained for communal spending will depress economic growth and make everyone the poorer.

There is no doubt that introducing the system will cause some economic disruption, but this is the consequence of the imposition of taxation in the first place. One cannot blame these problems on removal of an evil when it should not have needed to be removed. The extent of any problems will reflect how skilfully the introduction of the system is handled. It will be a considerable test of the ability of the civil service.

It should be understood that taxation is continuing to cause distortion and reduced income in the economy and there is no virtue in prolonging this. Temporary disruption is not an adequate excuse for permanently keeping people poorer than they could be.

The benefits of the system are a larger, stronger, more productive economy with more earnings to be shared. There will also be a basic income for every person, separate from any earned by employment, which will help reduce poverty caused by economic factors. It will be people's reward for allowing businesses and consumers to use resources owned by the people for gain.

People will keep their income. None will be taken and misallocated by the state. They will mostly be able to provide for themselves because their income is their own to spend. The state and each of its levels of government will have to earn their income, from selling the use of resources, just as everyone else has to earn a living from their labour and investments. Taking taxes by coercion is far too easy a resort for governments. It is time it came to an end.

The economy will enjoy a considerable stimulus when the system is introduced, output will increase, though inflation is a temporary risk in the early days. Resources will be properly conserved and managed. Market failures in the use of common pool resources can be corrected and those for education and medical services substantially reduced, if not completely, eradicated. Government will be reduced to the collection of resource rentals and management of central services. People will no longer have to rely on untrustworthy governments for the provision of pensions and other necessities.

All these benefits make the case for the abolition of taxation irresistible. Thus, a resource dividend system of public finance has three fundamental effects.

First, people keep what they earn, instead of having a great part of it taken under threat of suffering at the hands of the state. As they can choose for themselves how they spend the money it will be used more efficiently, creating a single but permanent stimulus to the economy. There will also be a further improvement in the economy, likewise single but permanent, arising from the removal of the deadening impact of taxation on companies and investment.

Secondly, the income generated by the economy will be shared on the principle of equal ownership of the resources of the world. It is unlikely that those who are currently rich will be significantly worse off. The poor will not become rich but they will be better off.

Finally, the resources of the earth will for the first time be properly managed and conserved.